"I can only imagine the number of marriages that will be saved or strengthened by this helpful book. Grief pummels even the strongest marriage. I've felt it. My wife and I battled the waves of sorrow that kept crashing on our home, and I wish we had had this book, with its combination of biblical truth and practical counsel, as a resource during our painful journey."

MARK VROEGOP, Lead Pastor, College Park Church, Indianapolis; Author, *Dark Clouds, Deep Mercy*

"What a great gift for any married couple that experiences what one hymnwriter called the 'frowning providence' of God. From their own experience, Jeff and Sarah are able to show us that even on dark days God is good, and that he can be trusted."

BOB LEPINE, Host, FamilyLife Today

"Jeff and Sarah have firsthand understanding of suffering and trials in marriage. Like dear friends, they offer words of deep sympathy and understanding for painful circumstances, yet bring hope through timeless biblical truth. Whether your marriage is in a season of crisis or you're looking to fortify it for the unknown days ahead, this book is a gift."

LAURA WIFLER, Co-founder, Risen Motherhood; Co-author, *Risen Motherhood: Gospel Hope for Everyday Moments*

"I've ministered to hurting wives for many years, desiring to encourage them with the gospel in the midst of painful marital storms. I've discussed a variety of books with them, but none have accomplished what Jeff and Sarah have done with *Together Through the Storms*. They have masterfully shared their story of incredible suffering in a way that leads the reader to feel they are trustworthy friends, wise alongside-you encouragers, and humble followers of Jesus. This book is a gem! Don't just read it; savor it."

ELLEN DYKAS, Harvest USA; Author, *Sexual Sanity for Women*

"Sarah and Jeff are writing while life is still hard, and they talk about *your* storms. The only problem is this: you will not be able to give this book to your friends because you and your spouse will keep going back to the prayers at the end of each chapter. If couples pray those prayers together, they will be transformed."

ED WELCH, Counselor, CCEF; Author, *When People Are Big and God Is Small* and *Side by Side*

"Jeff and Sarah know what it is to live life under seemingly constant pressure. In this book they apply hard-won insights and biblical wisdom that will encourage you to cling a little tighter, not just to one another but ultimately to Christ. Reading it was a blessing—there was plenty of underlining going on!"

RACHEL WILSON, Co-author, *The Life We Never Expected*

"Jeff and Sarah Walton share their experiences with job loss, chronic illness, past emotional wounds, depression, intimacy, identity, and children, and show how God remains faithful through it all. The questions, prayers, and Scriptures at the end of each chapter will encourage open communication with your spouse and remind you that you are not alone in your storms, and to hold on to hope and stay the course. Your best days are ahead."

KIRK CAMERON, Actor; Producer

"Marriage is a wonderful gift from God, but it can be a place of excruciating pain. Jeff and Sarah know what it is to find hope in the midst of heartache. The fruit of this hope is found in this extremely helpful book. In an honest, sensitive and biblically faithful way, they encourage us to find courage in God. Sooner or later you will face trials. This book will help you to put your faith in the right place."

PAUL AND EDRIE MALLARD, Pastor, Widcombe Baptist Church, Bath, UK; Author, *Invest Your Suffering*

"This book does not offer an idealized view of marriage but rather a vulnerable account of failures, fears, and doubts, and a wonderful view of the God who strengthens us through them. This is remarkable wisdom that offers true help and hope for couples walking through suffering."

VANEETHA RISNER, Author, *The Scars That Have Shaped Me*

"When we say our vows, we don't really expect to face the tough part of the equation. So painful circumstances can cause stress fractures in even the strongest marriage. Jeff and Sarah know from experience what it is to walk this path. Their counsel goes beyond empty platitudes and points readers to a true source of help and hope. Wise, solid, and practical, this book is a lifeline."

MARY KASSIAN, Author, *The Right Kind of Strong*

"This raw and vulnerable book shines such hope and truth into all our lives, and into our marriages and families. This will be a real blessing to anyone experiencing trials."

PAUL AND RACHEL DALE, Senior Pastor, Church by the Bridge, Sydney, Australia

"Sarah and Jeff invite us into their hearts in the most humbling and helpful way. Be prepared to see yourself in these pages and, more importantly, to see Christ."

JON AND QUINA ARAGON, Co-owner, Native Supply / Author, *Love Made*

"Fresh, insightful, and engaging. While still in the trenches, Jeff and Sarah have found hope and togetherness where others have been overwhelmed by division and despair. This book will help you to see what's possible when two people facing troubles sincerely seek the help of Christ."

COLIN S. SMITH, Senior Pastor, The Orchard Evangelical Free Church, Arlington Heights, Illinois; President, Unlocking the Bible

"A large part of marriage counseling is helping couples journey through suffering. The questions, prayers, and suggested Scriptures make this book a ready resource for anyone needing hope when the light seems dim."

JONATHAN HOLMES, Pastor of Counseling, Parkside Church, Chagrin Falls, Ohio; Author, *Counsel for Couples*

"A phenomenal book that will encourage, challenge, and give hope. Every page will remind you that Christ is with you through rough waters. Every couple should have a copy!"

MARK AND LAURA PRICE, Four-time NBA All-Star, 1994 Dream Team II

"Offers sound scriptural wisdom for persevering through the hard things that come to every marriage at some point in the real world. Jeff and Sarah winsomely encourage couples to set a course for long-term joy in spite of sorrow, long-term contentment in spite of disappointment, and long-term hope in anticipation of ultimate restoration."

NANCY GUTHRIE, Bible teacher; Author, *Even Better Than Eden*

"A rare gift—empathy, biblical insight, honesty, and practical help for trials. This is a resource every marriage needs."

RUTH CHOU SIMONS, Author, *GraceLaced* and *Beholding and Becoming*

"A beautiful, courageous, and wise book. Whether you've had an easy marriage or a difficult one, please read this book! You won't find easy answers, but something better— the inspiring story of a married couple determined to honor God and love each other through all of life's hardships."

GARY THOMAS, Author, *Sacred Marriage* and *Cherish*

"Honest and transparent, this unique book will support and strengthen any marriage that needs to weather storms."

CAMERON COLE, Author, *Therefore I Have Hope*

JEFF & SARAH WALTON

Together Through *the* Storms

Biblical Encouragements
for Your Marriage
When Life Hurts

Together Through the Storms
© Jeff and Sarah Walton, 2020

Published by:
The Good Book Company

thegoodbook.com | www.thegoodbook.co.uk
thegoodbook.com.au | thegoodbook.co.nz | thegoodbook.co.in

ISBN: 9781784984724 | Printed in India

Design by André Parker

CONTENTS

Foreword

Robert Wolgemuth & Nancy DeMoss Wolgemuth

When I (Robert) and my late wife moved to central Florida, we quickly discovered that it's not a matter of if but when those dreaded seasonal hurricanes will hit. They can't be avoided. But neither do they have to catch us off guard. Bobbie and I learned how to take necessary precautions before the storms came, what to do in the midst of the high-velocity winds and torrential rains, and how to handle clean-up and any necessary repairs after the storm had passed through.

When it comes to the storms of life—whether literal or metaphorical—it's not a matter of if but when they will hit. We (Nancy and Robert) have seen this time and time again, both in our own lives and in the lives of others. Jesus himself told us this would be the case. The rain will fall, the floods will come, and the winds will blow and beat on our house and on yours (see Matthew 7 v 24-27).

When these storms assault those of us who are married, the structure of our relationship and home can sustain collateral damage—or, by the mercy and grace of God, it can become even stronger.

Thankfully, the One who created the rain and the wind—the One who commands and raises the stormy wind and who, when it pleases him, makes the storm be still (Psalm 107 v 25, 29)—has not left us to weather life's tempests on our own. He has given us everything we need to build our homes on the kind of foundation that will keep them from falling when the storms beat upon them.

Over the course of sixteen years of marriage, Jeff and Sarah Walton have been pummeled by one storm after another; seemingly relentless gale-force winds and driving rains have whipped up against their family, causing them at times to feel tossed about and in danger of going under. But through those tumultuous times—in part, *because* of those storms—their faith and their marriage have become even more steadfast and secure.

From the crucible of their own story, this volume unpacks the unvarnished truth about dashed dreams and expectations, and, as you'll discover, about the hope that results from clinging tightly to Christ and his word, even as the storms lash against us from every side.

The book (or the electronic device) that you hold in your hand contains wisdom and encouragement that virtually every couple will need along the way—because it simply is not possible to be married for any length of time and not face, sooner or later, circumstances that threaten to overwhelm you. Jeff and Sarah speak candidly about disappointed hopes, depression, standing by each other when your children suffer, navigating the heartbreak of prodigal children, facing chronic illness, issuing forgiveness, embracing humility, dealing with the challenges that suffering can create with a couple's intimacy, and much more.

The essence of this book is relentlessly practical, yet these pages are filled with the overarching theme that a better marriage is not the ultimate goal. Knowing Christ more intimately is what Jeff and Sarah offer as the outcome supremely worth holding on for. We agree. In the midst of turbulent seasons, if we turn to Christ rather than turn against each other, then by God's grace our lives and marriages can be strengthened through the storms, rather than destroyed by them.

For us, one of the "money" paragraphs in this book (and there are many) is this:

> *Hard as it is to remember this when the storms hit, our suffering is never our greatest problem—our sin is. And our sin is what God has dealt with, fully and finally, through the sacrificial death and triumphant resurrection of Jesus Christ.*

This is the gospel—the hope we have not only for eternal salvation but for each and every moment of our lives.

With all the demands and obligations that you surely face in your marriage and (if you have one) your family, reading a book together can be a challenge. We get that. But we've done this a few times, and it's been well worth the effort. If you'll allow us to be so presumptuous, may we recommend that you and your spouse take the time to read this one—together. Our prediction is that you will be encouraged and blessed.

If you're currently in the swirl of a stormy season, this resource may prove to be a life-saver. If you are in a season of relative calm, it will prepare you to face the inevitable storms that lie ahead. And if past storms have caused damage to your heart and your marriage, you will find help for the clean-up and restoration process, and for shoring up the foundations before further storms arise. There are no marriages we know about—including our own—that could not use this book to great advantage.

Thank you, Jeff and Sarah, for pouring out this "love offering" for friends like us, and for others who will read your words and receive an infusion of hope for the hard times.

And may God bless you, the reader, as you anchor your life and marriage on the solid Rock of Jesus Christ and his word.

Robert Wolgemuth & Nancy DeMoss Wolgemuth

JEFF AND SARAH WALTON live in Chicago with their four children. They are members of The Orchard Evangelical Free Church in Arlington Heights. Sarah is the co-author of *Hope When It Hurts* and you'll find her online at setapart.net and @Swalts4.

Introduction

We remember it like it was yesterday. The sun was shining, everyone was smiling, and, other than the fact that the DJ played the wrong song for our first dance (which we eventually laughed about), it was as close to a perfect day as it's possible to be. I was twenty-three. She was twenty. Sarah and I were young, we were in love, we were excited, and we were ready (or so we thought) to embark on a life together.

We didn't expect life to be perfect, of course—but we naturally assumed our marriage would be filled with more of the "better" than the "worse." So with stars in our eyes and big dreams for what the future would hold, we confidently vowed:

> *"I take you … to have and to hold, from this day forward, for better or for worse, for richer or for poorer, in sickness and in health, for as long as we both shall live."*

That was nearly sixteen years ago. Little did we know that those years would bring chronic illness, financial loss, job loss, special needs, suffering children, overwhelming stress, and the marital strain that accompanies each. We never imagined that we'd experience so much of the "worse," "poorer," and "in sickness" parts of our vows.

The reality is that all marriages pass through storms; every husband and wife has a story to tell of a marriage that includes some happy parts, some funny parts, and some hard and painful parts. There are times of calm, when everything sails along serenely; and there are the storms, when you wonder how to keep the water out of your boat—or whether you'll even stay afloat. And we're guessing that you've picked up this book because you're either in a storm of your own right now, and maybe your marriage needs encouragement or help, or because you want to prepare your marriage for the storms that may lie ahead.

The great news is that no marriage (including yours) is beyond hope, and every marriage (including yours) can be strengthened—even by the storms.

We know this is true not only in theory but in reality— because it's our reality.

OUR STORY

Less than three years into our marriage, we excitedly welcomed our first child into the world. All was going well until he spiked a fever and was hospitalized with a severe infection at seven weeks old. After five days in the hospital with terrifying, inconclusive reports, we were sent home without answers. We thought it was an isolated incident, but over time it turned into years of life-altering neurological challenges that have forever changed our family's lives. Every day, we helplessly watched as our sweet, smart, funny little boy would turn into someone else, displaying behavior that was extremely difficult to control and navigate. Countless consultations, tests, and evaluations left doctors shaking their heads, and all we were left with in the end was an increased financial burden, a stressful home life, and growing fears for him and us.

Along with that, Sarah's health was rapidly declining, and with each of our four children that she bore, she was increasingly unable to function through her own chronic pain and illness. On top of that, an ankle injury that she sustained in high school has now led to five surgeries and an inability to do much of what she loves anymore.

As our son's disorder continued to intensify, and as Sarah grew sicker and our younger children began to exhibit their own chronic pains, my job as a consultant to orthopedic surgeons often kept me from being home. Our marriage began to suffer under the weight of it all.

In 2015, we were led to a group of doctors who connected Sarah's many symptoms to Lyme disease and, over the following year, the growing symptoms in each of our children led to testing that revealed the illness had been passed on to each one of them. The medical community gave us conflicting advice and very little support, but the growing neurological and physical ailments in each of our children were impossible to deny, and became increasingly confusing and expensive to navigate.

We were at our lowest point, and convinced that we couldn't endure anything else, and so it became clear that I could no longer sustain my on-call job. So I left it behind, along with half of our income. We sold our dream home and downsized to a smaller rental home.

A year later, my new company began to struggle and suddenly I was without a job—leaving us with no income at all.

Our family was in crisis. Most of our time spent together as a couple consisted of doctor appointments, navigating challenges with our son, soothing crying and hurting children, discussing what treatments we could afford, healing from each of the nine surgeries undergone between the two of us, dealing with Sarah's chronic pain, and stressing about our draining finances, all the while being too exhausted to address the tensions that were building within our marriage. We were both broken and both wondering where God was and why he was allowing such deep and layered suffering. As we endured one loss after another, we found ourselves battling despair and hopelessness, and being confronted with deep questions of faith that neither of us had faced before. We were surviving, but we—and our marriage—were hanging on by a thread.

But we're still here. Still together. And, somehow, stronger for it all.

God held us up and enabled us not only to survive, but to see the good gifts he had given us along the way. Though it's been harder than we ever imagined, there have also been moments of laughter, sweet memories, and undeserved gifts. Somehow, in each moment of each day, God has helped us press on, has held our marriage together when we haven't had the strength to fight for it ourselves, and has taught us to find joy, even within the sorrow. And by his grace, he continues to hold us up each and every day, despite many of our circumstances remaining the same.

THE BIRTH OF A BOOK

A few years back, I (Sarah) co-wrote *Hope When It Hurts* while our family was enduring many of these same trials. By God's grace, it reached more people than we ever imagined it would, and changed more lives than we had dared hope. *Hope When It Hurts* dealt with suffering and faith on an individual level, but not with how suffering impacts our marriages, the relationship that can provide the greatest comfort and also cause the greatest pain. Despite being in the midst of our own storms, God put it on our hearts to write from this place of pain and hope to encourage other married couples who are facing storms of their own (or one day will). We wanted to write to remind you, whoever you are and however you came to this book, that you are not alone, that there is more to your suffering than meets the eye, and that, through Christ, whatever has happened or may happen, there is always hope for your marriage.

As we prayed about embarking on writing this book, during one of the hardest seasons of our life, our wise pastor and friend, Colin Smith, encouraged and counseled us with these words from Psalm 118 v 13-14, which became a truth that we hope to communicate throughout these pages:

> *I was pushed hard, so that I was falling,*
> *but the LORD helped me.*
> *The LORD is my strength and my song;*
> *he has become my salvation.*

We, and our marriage, have been pushed hard—sometimes to the point where we have felt as though we're falling. In fact, many days we feel as if we're falling once again. Our marriage has not been and is not perfect. We're writing in the trenches, right there beside you, not from the mountaintop. But we have written these pages as a testimony to the faithfulness, goodness, and sustaining grace of Jesus. He has been and continues to be our help, strength, song, and salvation.

So this is a book about marriage, but it's very different than most books on marriage. It's for the storms—to prepare you for them in the future, or to help you navigate them in the present, or to help you deal with the aftermath of what you've just come through. We hope to encourage you by acknowledging many (though certainly not all) of the challenges that we can face when storms come into and against our marriage. That's not because we've navigated our storms and safely reached the other side, but because Jesus Christ has been faithful to strengthen us, carry us, and change us and our marriage as we continue to weather them together.

Every marriage begins in the sun; every marriage must pass through storms. For you, maybe those storms have brewed within your marriage—from rubbing up against each other's weaknesses, differences, and sins—perhaps from the pain of infidelity, addiction, hurtful patterns of sin, or an unbelieving spouse. Or maybe for you it's been the storms of circumstances around your marriage: the experience of excitement over starting or growing a family becoming a deeply painful struggle with infertility, loss of a child, or special needs; or living with chronic illness, a life-altering injury, something that was done to you in the past, financial loss, tensions in your extended family, or a rebellious child.

Whatever your storms have been, or will be, these trials will inevitably cause you to wrestle with difficult and complex questions of faith—and they will either drive you closer together or further apart. It's where and to whom we turn to for the strength and hope that we need to endure the storms that will make all the difference.

These questions and the answers to them are why we have looked to the book of Job as the foundation of each chapter. Job—the story of a man who lost everything—may seem like an odd choice for a marriage book! But it contains truths that have taught us to worship, hope, grieve, lament, confess, and wrestle, and ultimately to come to see Jesus more clearly and love him more dearly, growing us to see each other better and love each other more in the process.

You can read your way through the whole book or go through its chapters in any order; you can read one a day or go more slowly (or quickly). It's written in such a way that it can be read as a couple or read on your own if that's more appropriate right now. You can work through it individually or with a group, and spend time engaging with the reflection questions, prayer, and further meditations at the end of each chapter.

Brother, sister, we wrote this book for you, not because we have all the answers but to point you to the hope you can have in Christ. It's through that hope, and the truths found throughout God's word, that you can find strength for the storms that come into and against your marriage. We're realistic. Storms will come. But we're full of hope. As we look to Christ and his word, we can, by God's grace, walk through the heaviest weather together—and find ourselves stronger in the storms.

CHAPTER 1

Our Hope in Life
and Marriage

I know that you can do all things, and that no
purpose of yours can be thwarted. I had heard of you
by the hearing of the ear, but now my eye sees you;
therefore I despise myself and repent in dust and
ashes. (Job 42 v 2, 5-6)

Who are we to write a book on marriage? We have a far-from-perfect marriage—and some days, it doesn't even reach that yardstick!

Those were the first things that came to mind when we thought of writing this book. Yet as we continued to pray, we realized that what we wanted to write about was not our own sufficiency or wisdom but the goodness, faithfulness, and sufficiency of Christ when everything in life—including your marriage—is being tested and tried.

So our approach toward this book will look different than many marriage books. Our aim is not to offer a "how to" guide on having the best marriage but rather to walk alongside of you and your spouse, sharing the realities of suffering and the effects it can have on marriage, but then lifting our eyes above our trials, off of our spouse, and onto our all-sufficient Savior.

If you and your spouse are in a different place spiritually right now—or maybe even on a different planet—here's the good news: Your relationship with Christ and your ability to honor him are not dependent on your spouse. Quite the opposite, actually: your relationship with your spouse is dependent on your relationship with Christ.

So that is where we must begin and where we must keep our eyes fixed as we navigate the storms of this life and the pressures they place on our marriages. Our hope needs to be not in our marriage—in what it is, or was, or may one day become—but in Christ alone. And the wonderful truth that we've learned is that when our hope is in Christ, there is always hope for every marriage.

LEARNING FROM JOB

Because of the nature and length of the trials we have experienced since the beginning of our marriage 16 years ago, we have often taken comfort from the life of Job, and it's his life that provides the framework for this book. If Job teaches us anything, it is that there is more to suffering than meets the eye. We'll see that in Job chapter 1—but before we get there, we're going to begin at the end of the book.

Job knew trials. He lost his livestock, camels, and servants (in other words, his wealth and his livelihood); he lost every one of his ten children in a single day; he was struck with horrific sores from head to toe; and, as if that weren't enough, his friends were convinced he had brought it all upon himself.

Understandably, Job's suffering was so crushing that he longed for death and pleaded with God to make known the cosmic reason behind his torment (Job 23). And yet, after wrestling with his friends' accusations, his unrelenting misery, and, finally, with God himself, Job came to this conclusion:

> *I know that you can do all things, and that no*
> *purpose of yours can be thwarted … I had heard of*

*you by the hearing of the ear, but now my eye sees
you. (Job 42 v 1, 5)*

Job's life ended with an amazing picture of redemption, restoration, and healing (including wealth, children, and friendships). We aren't promised a "happily ever after" in an earthly sense, but all those who follow the risen Jesus are promised an "inheritance that is imperishable, undefiled, and unfading, kept in heaven for you" (1 Peter 1 v 4). Yet our hope isn't only in the eternal happiness and healing to come, but in the blessing of experiencing what Job did—of seeing and knowing our God more, even in—especially in—our darkest days. It was in the midst of his deepest suffering, and not after it, that Job came to see God—to know him, to experience him, to marvel at him. Through what was—to him—inexplicable suffering, he came to grasp "the greatness, majesty, sovereignty, and independence of God" (John MacArthur Study Bible, notes on Job 42 v 6).

Our prayer is that as we press on with a future hope of better days to come, we will not miss the life-changing blessings that Christ has in store for us right in the midst of our suffering.

WHY WE NEED JESUS

So this is where it starts, as it did for Job: we need not only to know about Jesus, but to know that we need Jesus.

*And you were dead in the trespasses and sins in which
you once walked, following the course of this world,
following the prince of the power of the air, the spirit
that is now at work in the sons of disobedience—
among whom we all once lived in the passions of our
flesh, carrying out the desires of the body and the*

mind, and were by nature children of wrath, like the rest of mankind. But... (Ephesians 2 v 1-4a)

Saved and loved we may be, but we still sin. So, despite the "perfect-marriage face" most people put on each Sunday morning and when they're with friends, our marriages are going to be sites of struggle as well as joy, because all our marriages are made up of two sinners. Tension and problems will blow up on good days—and when storms come to two sinners in the same boat, we're often more tempted to push each other off the boat than help each other bail out water.

So, whatever else happens to us, we need to cling to the "But" at the start of verse 4:

But God, being rich in mercy, because of the great love with which he loved us, even when we were dead in our trespasses, made us alive together with Christ—by grace you have been saved—and raised us up with him and seated us with him in the heavenly places in Christ Jesus, so that in the coming ages he might show the immeasurable riches of his grace in kindness toward us in Christ Jesus. For by grace you have been saved through faith. And this is not your own doing; it is the gift of God, not a result of works, so that no one may boast. For we are his workmanship, created in Christ Jesus for good works, which God prepared beforehand, that we should walk in them. (Ephesians 2 v 4-10)

Hard as it is to remember this when the storms hit, our suffering is never our greatest problem—our sin is. And our sin is what God has dealt with, fully and finally, through the sacrificial death and triumphant resurrection of Jesus Christ. This is the gospel—the hope we have not only for eternal salvation, but for each and every moment of our lives.

This is what Job realized—that most of all he needed to see and trust God—the God who was far greater than him, whose plans were far beyond him, and whose designs for him were far better than his finite mind could understand.

It's seeing God and our need of him that makes our marriages into stable vessels, able to withstand storms even as we are being tossed about by them. If, as you read this, you feel hopeless—about your inability to change your own heart and love your spouse in the way God calls you to, or your inability to forgive and move forward, or your inability to withstand everything that life, or God, is throwing at you as a couple right now—we want to encourage you to bring your disappointments and hurts and inabilities to Jesus. By faith, ask Jesus to open the eyes of your heart to see him more clearly and know his life-changing power.

A FUTURE-LOOKING HOPE

We recently heard one of our former pastors, Bev Savage, give a powerful testimony of God's faithfulness amid the many heartbreaking circumstances throughout his life. He reflected on his experience of walking toward Michelangelo's famous statue of David in the Accademia Gallery in Florence, Italy. As you walk toward David, you walk past striking, partially-finished sculptures known as Michelangelo's Prisoners. As one site describes it:

> *"All the unfinished statues at the Accademia reveal*
> *Michelangelo's approach and concept of carving.*
> *Michelangelo believed the sculptor was a tool*
> *of God, not creating but simply revealing the*
> *powerful figures already contained in the marble.*
> *Michelangelo's task was only to chip away the excess,*
> *to reveal."* (www.accademia.org/explore-museum/
> artworks/michelangelos-prisoners-slaves)

"This striking image," Bev noted, "often comes to mind as I think of God as our sovereign Sculptor, little by little chiseling his children into the image of his Son. Rather than thinking, 'Why is this happening to me?' I think, 'What excess is he chipping off of me in order to reveal more of Jesus?'"

Though the blows are often painful and it's hard to see their purpose, we can trust the hand of our almighty Sculptor, who promises that he is using each painful stroke of his chisel to accomplish his loving eternal purposes for us and reveal more of the image of Christ within us. If it were up to us, we would stay a comfortable, shapeless block of marble! But our heavenly Father loves us too much to keep us as we are. For we are God's workmanship; having saved us through Christ, he chisels us into Christ-shaped people (Ephesians 2 v 10). And it's clear to us, looking back, that one of God's chisels is our marriage. He's used it to chip away, to reshape, and to refine—and that's often painful but always good. And we know he's not done yet!

If Jesus is Lord of your life, then let this be your perspective on the marriage he has given you and the storms he is leading you through. Nothing in your life—no grievous losses, no perplexing circumstance, no marital struggles—will fall to the ground as useless. Every moment of them is chipping away, gradually revealing more and more the glorious image of Christ.

Christian, one day we will stand in glory, and our eyes really will see Jesus. Sin, suffering, and struggle will be no more, and we will look back in awe and amazement and comprehension at all that seemed so confusing and devastating. What joy we will have when our faith becomes sight and we see how the kind and skilled hand of our heavenly Father chose us as his own, and faithfully worked to reveal in us the image of his Son—for his glory and our eternal joy in his presence.

The almighty Sculptor
promises that he is
using each stroke of his
chisel to accomplish his
loving purposes for us.

REFLECT

- Have you put your faith in Jesus Christ as your Lord and Savior? If not, how might the truth of the gospel change your sense of hope, both for today and eternity? If you're a Christian, how does the gospel change your suffering and your perspective on marriage even when challenges arise?
- What do you hope to take from this book? In what ways do you think you most need God to help you or change you as an individual?
- (Together, if possible) What trials are putting pressure on your marriage? Do you believe that Christ can use these trials for the good of your marriage? Why/why not? How have you seen him chisel each of you to make you more like Jesus?

PRAY

Lord, thank you that nothing in my life is hopeless because you laid down your life for me, offering forgiveness, freedom, and eternity with yourself. You see my sufferings and know the hidden places of my heart and marriage that need to be renewed, healed, and redeemed. Help me trust that you have purposes beyond what I can see and that nothing is impossible for you. Help me lay down what I think is best and submit my desires for my life, family, and marriage to you. I believe that you are worth following, no matter the cost, but help me believe this more deeply. Thank you for your grace and forgiveness when I live in fear instead of faith, selfishness instead of sacrificial love, and pride instead of humility before you and others. In the weeks ahead, open my eyes to the truth of your word, and chisel what you must to reveal more of your image within me. Amen.

For further meditation: Psalm 130; 1 Corinthians 1 v 26-31; Ephesians 1 v 16-21; Hebrews 12 v 1-2, 3-13.

Journaling

_____

_____

_____

_____

_____

_____

_____

_____

_____

_____

_____

_____

_____

_____

_____

_____

_____

_____

_____

_____

_____

CHAPTER 2

When Trials Come

*Then Satan ... said, "Does Job fear God for no
reason? Have you not put a hedge around him and
his house and all that he has, on every side? ...
Stretch out your hand and touch all that he has,
and he will curse you to your face." And the LORD
said to Satan, "Behold, all that he has is in
your hand." (Job 1 v 8-12)*

Trials—from small annoyances to seasons of deep suffering—will test every marriage. But not every marriage
will be shaped by them in the same way. The mark these
trials leave on us ultimately depends upon our response
when they come. An old saying goes, "The same sun that
melts the wax hardens the clay"—the same circumstances
that produce in one person resentment, bitterness, and
anger toward God and their spouse will in another person
end up strengthening their marriage and growing humility,
patience, kindness, and greater dependence on Christ.

The book of Job opens with a disagreement in the heavens
about how Job would react to a sustained season of deep
trial. Satan expected him to curse God when his earthly
blessings were removed. He was right—not about Job but
about his wife, who advised Job to do just what Satan was
aiming for (2 v 9-10). But Job ignored her advice and defied
Satan's expectations by clinging to his belief that God was,

somehow, working for good: "When he has tried me, I shall come out like gold" (23 v 10).

Don't miss what Satan was doing. In plunging this couple into turmoil, he was aiming to divide them from each other and then drag them from God. Job lost everything and then faced losing his marriage. And often so will we, when trials and testing come. Storms will shape your marriage—but *how* they shape it depends on your response to them and to each other. So here are three key truths to remember when they come.

YOUR SPOUSE IS NOT YOUR ENEMY

There have been times when I have viewed Sarah as my enemy (though at the time I wouldn't have said that out loud or written it in a book). Because we process our trials differently, especially when we are both carrying overwhelming stress loads, it's all too easy to take our frustrations out on each other. What used to be nothing more than minor annoyances are suddenly magnified when fears, disappointments, and hurts press us from all sides.

Instead of coming together as a united front to face our trials, we are tempted to retreat into our own little worlds or turn against each other in our pain. It's easy to end up pulling against rather than for our spouse and to allow our feelings to trump their needs.

And when we turn our spouse into the enemy, we become unaware of the true enemy that both of us are up against.

Picture a couple standing in their kitchen during the middle of the day. They're tired, worn out, and arguing about whether or not a family vacation can fit into the budget this year. Suddenly, an intruder breaks in and begins grabbing their most prized possessions, including their wedding photo album. In response, this couple completely ignore the intruder and go right on bickering. Eventually, a reluctant truce is called over the vacation. Sometime later, both of them separately wonder where various items from their home have gone.

No one would let that happen! At the point the intruder enters, arguing about a vacation would suddenly seem ridiculous. A far greater threat stands before that couple. Yet we often act in a similar manner. We feel the pressure on our lives and turn against each other in our discomfort (sometimes over the most minor things), all while an invisible (but very real) enemy is hard at work to destroy our marriage, turn us against our Lord, and rob us of the gold that God wants to refine in us as we trust in him. It's easy in the midst of pain or disappointment to give little attention to the spiritual battle that is being waged, and too much attention to our differences and unmet expectations.

Satan's purpose in attacking Job was to prove that Job only loved God for his earthly blessings rather than for God himself. Today, Satan's mission remains the same. He wants to convince you to turn against God. His pathway to that can subtly lie in persuading you to turn against your spouse.

So we need to fight the temptation to turn against our husband or wife and see them as the enemy. We need to proactively counteract that mindset. How? You can take the initiative to do something kind, thoughtful, and generous for your spouse. Leave a note on the bathroom mirror that says something that you love or appreciate about them, or how you can see God working in their life. Take on a chore that usually falls to your wife or husband—for me, that might be taking the initiative to throw in a load of laundry or to plan and prepare a meal for the family. Before turning on the TV, take time to pray for, talk with, and listen to your spouse.

If you are anything like me, you will often not *feel* like serving or moving toward your spouse—but our feelings often follow our actions. So rather than giving opportunity for bitterness or resentment to take root, cut off those thoughts as soon as they appear, and instead think about how you can move toward your spouse today and remind them (and yourself!) that you are on each other's side.

GOD SETS THE BOUNDARIES

There is an equal and opposite danger to forgetting that Satan is our enemy—and that's forgetting that Satan is not in charge. He has only as much power as our sovereign God has allowed him. In Job 1 v 12, God gives Satan *permission* to attack his servant Job: "Behold, all that he has is in your hand. Only against him do not stretch out your hand." When Satan realizes that his attacks haven't achieved what he'd hoped, he returns to God and asks for more leash. The Lord replies, "Behold, he is in your hand; only spare his life" (2 v 6). While Satan took every liberty God gave him in his attempt to destroy Job's confidence in God's love and goodness, he could not go one step beyond the boundary line which God had determined.

Satan can go no further today than he could then. While we may wish that Satan had a much shorter leash and was given no room to do anything, we mustn't miss the point that the leash does exist, and it is held by God. He decides its length, for his own purposes. Satan is not in control.

Thomas Boston, the eighteenth-century preacher, explained this truth well when he wrote:

> "If God did not bind these crooks [undesirable circumstances], however painful they are in anyone's case, they would be even more so. But he says to the sinful instrument (whether Satan, our own

*sin, or living in a broken world) as He said to the
sea in creation, 'Thus far shall you come, and no
farther, and here shall your proud waves be stayed'
(Job 38:11) … Therefore, a crook of this kind is
never more or less grievous, but is exactly as God
determines it should be by his powerful bounding."
(The Crook in the Lot, modern English version
by Jason Roth, page 30)*

This truth can bring peace when circumstances seem
chaotic and trials feel unending. Though we may not
understand God's ways, we can be confident that all things
are within the good and sovereign bounds of our heavenly
Father. As C.H. Spurgeon, the nineteenth-century London
preacher, wrote:

*"The storm may rage, but all is well, for our Captain
is governor of storms. Courage, dear friend. The Lord,
the ever-merciful, has appointed every moment of
sorrow and every pang of suffering. If He ordains the
number ten, it can never rise to eleven, nor should
you desire that it shrink to nine. The Lord's time
is best. The span of your life is measured to a hair's
width. Restless soul, God ordains all, so let the Lord
have His way." (Beside Still Waters, page 143)*

Job lost almost everything, but he lost nothing more than
God allowed, and nothing more than what God knew would
be for his ultimate good. Hard though it is at times, we too
can—and need to—trust that everything is within the wise
bounds of our good and sovereign Lord.

GOD WILL USE THE ENEMY'S DEVICES

Did you notice who initiated the conversation about Job
in the exchange between Satan and God? It was God. He

knew exactly how this story would unfold, and he knows how ours will as well. When we find ourselves faced with trials, while feeling weary of the battle, we have to remember that our story isn't finished. We can look at what we can see—at what seems hopeless and impossible in the moment, at how it seems nothing good can come from our circumstances—or we can lift our eyes to a hope beyond what we can see.

But at this point you may be thinking, "Really? Why should I trust that God knows what he is doing, or wants good for me, when I am walking through *this*?"

Because of the cross.

The cross was the darkest moment in history, and it was God's initiative. God allowed his only Son to give more, and to lose more, than Job did or than you can—the riches of heaven, the worship of angels, and then even his own life in our place. If you want to see the moment of Satan's greatest apparent triumph, look here, at the cross, at the Son of God dying alone and in agony. And yet what looked like Satan's greatest triumph was in fact his ultimate defeat. Imagine Satan smirking as the Son of God was rejected, tortured, and led to the cross, only to find that his power was crushed at that cross, as Jesus bore the penalty for our sin and left Satan with nothing to accuse us of.

Yes, God used what Satan did in his Son's life for his purposes, for his Son's glory, for our good. Yes, he used what Satan did in Job's life for his good. And yes, he purposes to use all that happens to us for our good too (Romans 8 v 28).

I've seen this—I've lived it. The enemy has worked hard to knock Sarah and me down, both individually and as a couple. At times, it's appeared as if he's won. But as we look back, we see how God has not only carried us through but has used the enemy's tactics (along with our sin and suffering) to strengthen us and bring us closer to him.

It's not always easy to see (and honestly, I see far more of it in Sarah than in me), but we have begun to see the gold that God is forming through putting us through the fires.

Friend, I don't know what you're facing right now, but I know that God does. I don't know what the enemy has removed in order to tempt you to turn away from God by turning against your spouse, but I know the person you married is not your enemy but rather your companion. I know you're not in control right now, but I know that neither is Satan, because God is. I don't know what God is doing in you through your trials right now, but I know that he's at work, and I know it will be worth it as you cling to him and walk closely with your spouse (if they are willing). Why not, sometime today, look the person you married in the eye and tell them that you love them and that you're for them—and that God is too.

REFLECT

- In difficult times, are there ways in which you have placed blame on your spouse or allowed differences and annoyances to turn you against each other? When struggles arise within your marriage, do you ever consider that you have an enemy who is seeking to destroy anything that glorifies God, including our marriages? How would remembering the spiritual battle that is raging and the strong defender we have in Christ impact the disagreements, struggles, and circumstances within your marriage?
- How does understanding that God sets the boundaries give you comfort and hope, and change your current view of suffering?
- (Together, if possible) Can you recognize areas in your marriage where the enemy has sought (perhaps

successfully) to turn you against one another? What would it look like to resist him, asking Jesus to give you strength to stand firm and love one another?

PRAY

Lord Jesus, my heart is prone to wander, especially when times are difficult and painful, and the stresses of life seem to have no end. Search my heart, ground me in your truth, and give me clarity to see who my real enemy is. Help me to see where I have falsely accused or blamed my spouse (or others) for what we are enduring, and to realize that it may well be that my spouse is not the problem, but that the sin within me is. By the strength of your Holy Spirit, humble me now so that I may remember that my identity is found in you alone and not in my circumstances or in my spouse. Give me a renewed strength to fight and endure for your glory. Align our hearts together with yours and each other's, and may we rest in your promises that you are sovereign over our suffering. Use my life and my marriage for your kingdom's purposes and glory. Amen.

For further meditation: 2 Samuel 22 v 1-7; Psalm 18 v 16-19; 2 Corinthians 12 v 7-10; James 1 v 2-6.

Journaling

_____

_____

_____

_____

_____

_____

_____

_____

_____

_____

_____

_____

_____

_____

_____

_____

_____

_____

_____

_____

CHAPTER 3

How to Cling to Hope in Loss

Then Job arose and tore his robe and shaved his
head and fell on the ground and worshiped.
(Job 1 v 20-22)

When loss comes, grief is often not far behind. Though the shock of pain or the adrenalin of the survival instinct may make us appear strong for a time, grief—"the inward desolation that follows losing something or someone we loved" (J.I. Packer, *A Grief Sanctified*, page 9)—will eventually find its way into every fiber of our being.

Grief follows the great losses that some of us walk through (death, infertility, abuse, a wayward child, and so on), and it follows the smaller yet still painful losses (financial issues, missed opportunities, disappointments). All are hard to navigate in a marriage.

Job knew loss. He lost everything—his livestock, servants, and every one of his children. In one fell swoop, his wealth, security, and family were stripped away. Yet, in response to unfathomable affliction, Job does something equally unfathomable: he shaves his head, falls to the ground, and *worships the Lord.*

This is unfathomable because it is so different than the way most of us, including Christians, respond to trials.

In Western culture, we're often uncomfortable with grief, doing our best to avoid the reality that death and decay (of people and things) is evidence that this world is wasting away. Instead, we strive to appear strong, think positive, and fill our lives with whatever will help mask the pain. Or, instead of allowing grief and loss to drive them to a greater hope, many avoid facing brokenness head on by relieving the deep ache with whatever will dull the pain. Alternatively, sometimes as Christians we do grieve, but we think that while we grieve we can be excused from worshiping God—we'll start living for him again once we feel better and the grief has faded.

How can we learn to respond as Job did? And why would we even want to?

GRIEF IS NOT A SIGN OF UNBELIEF

Don't think that Job's worship was in place of his grief, or that those who believe do not feel grief at all. As the pastor and author John Piper points out:

> *"The sobs of grief and pain are not the sign of unbelief. Job knows nothing of a flippant, insensitive, superficial 'Praise God anyhow' response to suffering. The magnificence of his worship is because it was in grief, not because it replaced grief. Let your tears flow freely when your calamity comes. And let the rest of us weep with those who weep."*
>
> *(Job: Reverent in Suffering, desiringgod.org/ messages/job-reverent-in-suffering, accessed 12/1/19)*

It's natural and right to grieve the losses and pain we experience in this life. Grief and tears are not a sign of weak faith, but a normal and healthy response to the brokenness of this world and the painful effects that it has upon our lives. The Bible tells us that this fallen world is not the place we were designed for. The place we were made for is coming, but it is not here yet. Until then, we have to learn to live in a land between—grieving but hoping, unsettled in the pain but at peace in Christ's presence, worshiping in our pain.

Having hope doesn't mean we won't grieve. Having hope means we grieve with the confidence that "Christ will himself restore, confirm, strengthen, and establish you" (1 Peter 5 v 10).

THE UPS AND DOWNS OF WORSHIPING IN GRIEF

Equally, Job's worship did not mean his grief didn't continue. Job didn't, and we don't, walk through the pain of loss in a week or two, never to feel the absence or pain again. (The book of Job would be far shorter, but far less helpful and hopeful for us, if he had!) In truth, we typically don't feel the full weight of our grief until the shock wears off, the meals stop coming, our friends stop calling, and the world seems to move on while we are left with our pain and daily reminders of our loss.

Job didn't find it easy. He, like us, went up and down in his worship. By chapter 19, Job's words begin to sound far less worshipful:

> *Behold, I cry out, "Violence!" but I am not*
> *answered; I call for help, but there is no justice.*
> *[God] has walled up my way, so that I cannot pass,*
> *and he has set darkness upon my paths. He has*
> *stripped from me my glory and taken the crown*
> *from my head. He breaks me down on every side,*
> *and I am gone, and my hope has he pulled up like a*
> *tree. (Job 19 v 7-10)*

God doesn't expect us to be silent in our pain, grinning and bearing it. Grief and worship can co-exist, and so can trust and questions.

But Job isn't ceasing to worship; rather, the face of his worship has begun to change. Now Job reveals his trust in the Lord by honestly bringing his pain and confusion before him. Though it's wrong to grumble about God, we're allowed to come to him humbly and ask him, "Why?" and we're allowed to feel conflicted. God doesn't expect us to be silent in our pain, grinning and bearing it, but to come to him honestly, with all our questions, fears, hurts, and confusion. It's here, in the unsettling place of grief, that we can wrestle with, and begin to understand, the depths of God's love and goodness toward us.

Grief and worship can co-exist, and so can trust and questions. Even as Job asks what God is doing, he reminds himself of what he knows:

> *I know that my Redeemer lives, and at last he will stand upon the earth. And after my skin has been thus destroyed, yet in my flesh I shall see God, whom I shall see for myself, and my eyes shall behold, and not another. (Job 19 v 25-27)*

When a fresh wave of grief comes, we let the tears come, we cry out to the Lord with honesty in our pain... and we remind ourselves of the hope of the gospel. Our grief acknowledges that things are not as they should be, while our hope in the gospel reminds us that our grief no longer tells the whole story. We have a Redeemer, who paid the price to set us free from the punishment for our sin and will one day set us free from the presence of sin. When he returns, he will redeem what has been lost and restore what has been broken. At last—and not a moment too soon as we struggle through our trials—he will stand upon the earth, and we will stand with him, beyond the loss and the grief and the pain and the death.

WALKING IN GRIEF WITH YOUR SPOUSE

Not long ago, as I was experiencing another wave of grief over trials that have plagued our family for years, I felt myself pulling away from Jeff. I felt lonely, and I felt resentful. It felt to me that he seemed completely untouched by all that was going on, while I was battling fresh heartache. One day, after believing the lies that he didn't care and was detached from the circumstances that felt (and still feel) so devastating to me, the dam of resentment I'd allowed to build up broke and I told him, in a forthright way, how I was feeling.

His response was calmer than my outburst, thankfully. He explained how he was struggling in his own way. It was a much-needed reminder that we are both grieving, but the face of our grief often varies. As I've reflected on that conversation, I've taken three things away that I need to remember:

1. PEOPLE GRIEVE DIFFERENTLY

Couples tend to grieve differently than each other, just as Jeff and I do. One of you may express grief through frequent bouts of tears and will need to talk things through; one of you may show little emotion at all, and you cope by distracting yourself with anything that will keep your mind elsewhere. One of you may feel as though you have to hold it together, and then months or years later your own grief suddenly and unexpectedly begins to surface. Recognize these differences and be patient with one another—and communicate with each other. One of the enemy's powerful attacks on a marriage is the words that should be spoken but never are. When a husband and wife do not communicate their grief and let the other one into their wrestling with God at the appropriate time, the "one flesh" can feel as though it has split into two.

2. YOUR SPOUSE ISN'T CHRIST

Remember to bring your grief first and foremost to Christ, for he alone is the source of your hope and strength. If you expect your spouse to be able to provide all the comfort you need, or to understand you fully and completely and respond with wisdom and just the right encouragement, you'll be disappointed and they'll be crushed, and you'll both grow resentful.

3. YOUR SPOUSE IS YOUR SPOUSE

Yes, your spouse is not your Savior, but they can share both your joy and pain in ways that others can't and weren't meant to. If we begin to think independently from each other, and we are unwilling to let our spouse into our heartache because we think they won't understand or may say the wrong thing, it's bound to leave us vulnerable to the enemy's attacks. In the end, our silence robs us of the opportunity and privilege to walk and grow alongside of each other, coming to know more of Christ together and grow more in love with each other through our suffering.

(Jeff) As a husband, it's tempting for me to take my pain solely to the Lord but then to keep it all from Sarah. When I do this, I sacrifice trust and intimacy between us. At times my motive may be one of not wanting to place any additional burden upon Sarah, but at others it is because I don't like to show weakness. I need to remember that we need to grieve *together*, even as we grieve differently. God wants me to knit my heart together with Sarah's, leading us both to stronger faith through greater dependency on and delight in our loving Savior. And I need to be open with Sarah if that is to happen.

WHAT IS MOST PRECIOUS HAS NOT BEEN LOST

How was Job able to respond in worship in the way he did? Not because he was not grieving his awful losses, but because he knew that what was most precious to him he had not lost and never could. If you know Jesus, you too can lose precious things yet still worship. Grief can refocus us on the value of Christ and the security we have in him. This is why grief and joy can co-exist and even grow together. To experience that alongside of our spouse is a gift we will only know if we're willing to let each other into the ups and downs of our grief, and extend grace to our spouse as they navigate the ups and downs of theirs—as messy and unpredictable as that can be.

Friends, it's ok to grieve, but don't grieve alone. Let Christ into it and know the joy he has for you. And let your spouse into it and know the closeness which that can bring. Unexpected blessings are found as we walk side by side on the path where joy and sorrow meet.

REFLECT

- How would you characterize the way you respond to grief? Does your spouse seem to grieve in a similar or different manner?
- Have you believed the lie that grief is a sign of unbelief? If so, how would things change if you allowed yourself to fully grieve, understanding that, like Job, you can worship the Lord in your sorrow?
- (Together, if possible) Share how your spouse can be an encouragement to you as you grieve the loss or pain you have experienced. Share with each other what has helped and what has hurt in regards to navigating your sorrow as a couple.

PRAY

Heavenly Father, thank you that you give us permission to grieve over the trials that you have allowed into our lives. Like Job, help me to come to you honestly about my heartache and to trust that you can handle my pain, questions, and wavering emotions. But help me not to get stuck there. Give me the strength and faith to grieve with hope and offer you a sacrifice of worship, trusting that you will one day bring full redemption and restoration to all that we have lost. Protect our marriage as we learn to grieve alongside of each other, and help us to grow together as we look to you in our sorrow. Amen.

For further meditation: Psalms 13, 88; 1 Thessalonians 4 v 13.

Journaling

CHAPTER 4

Holding All Things Loosely

The LORD gave, and the LORD has taken away;
blessed be the name of the LORD. (Job 1 v 21b)

Recently we drove past our old house for the first time since downsizing into a rental property four years ago. Immediately, our four children began rehearsing memories, listing out every part of the house they miss and, once again, struggling to understand why we had to give it all up.

I tried explaining that it was the right thing for our family to follow God's leading, even at the cost of financial comfort and a home we loved. But deep down, I wrestled with my own nostalgia and questions. Why *did* we have to give it all up?

Rewind six years...

WHEN THE PLANS ARE CHANGED

We were living well below our means, carefully planning for the future, and seeking wise counsel in regard to being good stewards of our rising income. I was working as a trauma consultant, supporting doctors in trauma surgeries as they implanted medical devices. Financially, life was good. Things were going, for the most part, according to plan. By which I mean, our plan.

It was right then that, in his strange sovereignty, God chose to teach us how little control we really had.

Our eldest child's neurological challenges were growing worse or more obvious, and they were starting to consume us. Other pressures were mounting too. Sarah's health continued to decline. The other kids started showing signs of health problems. My on-call job often left Sarah as a single parent. Tension in our marriage grew. Medical bills increased.

Life was not good. Things were not going to plan. I realized that our family was in crisis.

God led us to realize that the only option was to let go of all we had saved, planned, and worked hard for. I took a new job that allowed me to be home more often, at the cost of a significant portion of my previous salary. We sold our dream home and moved in with my in-laws. We started to adjust to the drastic change of income.

And then, a year later, my new company laid off the majority of its employees—including me. Suddenly, we were faced with overwhelming expenses and no income at all.

Where did we go wrong?

Maybe somewhere, but maybe nowhere.

I've thought of Job often during this hard season of loss, resonating a little with the agony he must have felt when a lifetime of honorable hard work was wiped away in moments. What I find it harder to identify with is his response: "The LORD gave, and the LORD has taken away; blessed be the name of the LORD" (Job 1 v 21b).

In essence, Job is saying, *Whatever we enjoy is from the Lord, and we bless him for it—and whatever we lose is also from the Lord, and we need to learn to bless him for that, too.*

But how do we learn to do that? How does our family drive past our old house and actually bless God that we don't have it anymore?! How can you learn to look back at what you've lost and say, "Blessed be the name of the Lord"?

It is so counter-intuitive and unnatural! Well, maybe that's precisely why God allows these losses in our lives—to challenge our short-term view of blessing and open our eyes to deeper and lasting blessings that only Christ can give.

We are naturally tempted to equate God's pleasure over us with the earthly blessings we receive—we live in a world where comfort and pleasures are often dictated by our financial status. But the Bible makes it clear that the value system of God's kingdom is far different than the world's. We need to learn that value system—and, if possible, to learn it as a couple. That way, we can remind each other, as we drive past our old house or remember whatever else it is that we once had and have now lost, that the Lord is good in what he gives, and the Lord is good in what he takes.

Through these painful years, God has taught Sarah and me to search our hearts by continually asking three questions.

1. DO I LIVE IN FEAR OF LOSING MY COMFORT?

The fear of the LORD leads to life,
and whoever has it rests satisfied;
he will not be visited by harm. (Proverbs 19 v 23)

If we desire worldly comforts and fear earthly loss more than we desire God, then we will likely make decisions and plans according to what we think will keep our lives most comfortable. Looking back, I can now see the Lord's severe mercy in overturning the plans we had set for our lives— even plans that were good and wise. He removed all of our means of finding comfort and security in this world. It was painful, yes, but it was also freeing.

As our eyes become increasingly fixed on fearing the Lord and trusting his promises for us, we can live in greater freedom to trust and follow God's plan, rather than living in bondage to our own.

2. WHAT AM I BUILDING?

It is worth reflecting regularly on what we are pouring our time, energy, and money into building. Am I working so hard to build a family that is financially secure and enjoys comfort and ease that they rarely see me? Am I providing my wife with everything money buys, but nothing that lasts forever? Am I giving my church my Sunday attendance, but so busy earning that they get nothing else?

Sarah and I have reflected on hard decisions we've made. Was it worth the cost? Had I not changed jobs, we would still be living in that house that we were sure we'd grow old in, with the luxuries that we once had. We would also be living in a hurting marriage, and it would be a house I was rarely in. We'd leave a legacy of wealth but not of love. So was the cost worth it? Yes, it undoubtedly was. Would we have ever chosen it if the Lord had not forced us to? I'm not sure we would.

Friends, no matter what your financial status is, does your lifestyle show that you are living as if this earth is your home? Do your decisions suggest that what your marriage and family need most is earthly wealth and comfort?

3. IS JESUS ENOUGH?

I have learned in whatever situation I am to be content. I know how to be brought low, and I know how to abound. In any and every circumstance, I have learned the secret of facing plenty and hunger, abundance and need. I can do all things through him who strengthens me. (Philippians 4 v 11-14)

In a two-year period we went from debating how to redesign and remodel our kitchen to wondering how we would feed our family of six on food stamps, and deciding which medical treatments we could not afford to wait on even though we had no money to pay for them. I found this so hard. I was the provider of our family, and now I was often having to say, "We just don't have the money to do that right now." I felt the weight and responsibility of digging us out of the hole that we were in. And yet I was also discovering that truly Christ was enough. He provided us with what we needed, and not what we wanted or thought we needed. And, most of all, he had saved us and was spiritually sustaining us. We had been brought low, and I learned there how to be content, regardless of circumstances. That's a hard lesson to learn, but a good one.

It's still not easy. We wrestled with trusting the Lord's leading when it seemed only to lead to greater need and suffering. We are tempted to envy the seemingly comfortable lives of those around us. We question why God would allow us to lose everything when we are earnestly seeking to honor him in our steps. We struggle to understand why God has taken away even provision for the necessary treatments and doctors that our family's chronic health issues require. Yet by his grace, he has continually shown himself faithful—providing in his way and timing, while changing our hearts along the way. And at times we need each other to remind ourselves of this, because on our own we're so apt to forget it.

As hard as it's been, I'm grateful that God has given us a taste of both abundance and need. He has used both extremes to show us that our joy and hope will never be secure if we are placing them in our immediate comforts or long-term plans, instead of enjoying what God gives as a gift from him, to bless him for—and accepting what God takes as a hard gift from him, to bless him for. In whatever

circumstances we find ourselves, we can honor the Lord by
being content with what he has provided for us today. Of
course we can make wise plans, save for the future, and seek
to steward our finances well. But it all may change tomorrow, and we have no need to fear—if we've learned that
Christ has been and will be enough. Christ is enough for
eternity, and so he is enough for today.

THE ROCKIER PATH IS THE BETTER ONE

> *They spend their days in prosperity, and in peace they*
> *go down to Sheol. They say to God, "Depart from us!*
> *We do not desire the knowledge of your ways."*
>
> *(Job 21 v 13-14)*

There is a different, easier road to take. It is a prosperous,
often peaceful walk on smooth ground downhill, all the
way to death and misery. But God loves his children far too
much to allow us short-term ease if it will lead to the loss of
eternal pleasures in his presence. When Sarah and I look at
the loss of our financial comfort in contrast to the joy and
contentment in Christ that we have gained in its place, we
can do nothing but thank God for his goodness toward us.
It is better to be on the rocky, difficult road, walking uphill
all the way to Christ. On that path lie difficult decisions,
and God will sometimes (often) lighten the load by taking
away things that we love but that he knows could weigh us
down. Yet on that path we are with Christ, and at the end
of that road lies seeing Christ face to face and blessing him
for all he gave and all he took away. It is good to walk that
road together, keeping each other looking forward when we
stumble—and, yes, telling our kids when we drive past our
old house that walking this path is worth it.

REFLECT

- Which of the three questions in the subheads in this chapter challenged you the most? Might God be revealing an area in which he desires to give you freedom and peace?
- Have you been thinking—perhaps without realizing— that God will bless you financially if you follow him? How does this skew your view of Jesus and the gospel?
- (Together, if possible) Discuss which questions challenged you the most. Is money an area that causes tension in your marriage? What might need to change in the way you think, or talk, or make decisions?

PRAY

Lord, I desire to honor you in our finances, but if I'm honest, it's easy to be anxious about what we need and fearful over what we might lose. Help us to enjoy and be wise and generous with what you have entrusted us with, but not to put our hope in worldly wealth. Help us communicate openly and graciously about the financial challenges we face. Search my heart and show me if there is anything I am placing my hope in, and show me also what it would look like to hope in you instead. By the power of your Spirit, would you go on changing both of our hearts to trust you completely. Amen.

For further meditation: Matthew 6 v 20; Matthew 25 v 14-30; 2 Corinthians 4 v 18; 1 Peter 4 v 10.

Journaling

_____

_____

_____

_____

_____

_____

_____

_____

_____

_____

_____

_____

_____

_____

_____

_____

_____

_____

_____

_____

_____

_____

_____

_____

_____

CHAPTER 5

Loving Your Spouse Through Chronic Illness

And he said, "Naked I came from my mother's womb, and naked shall I return. The LORD gave, and the LORD has taken away; blessed be the name of the LORD." (Job 1 v 21)

"Lord, I pray you will do a physical miracle in my wife, but if you choose not to, then work a spiritual miracle in me so that I can love her well until the end."

These were the words of Dr. Robertson McQuilkin, shortly after receiving his wife's Alzheimer's diagnosis. His response pierced my heart as if someone had reached into my soul and exposed a hidden place of fear and insecurity. *Will my husband be able to love me well until the end, even if our life is never free from the painful effects of chronic illness and the disabilities I face? Will he reach a point where the sacrifice becomes too great? Could I even blame him if he did?*

Not long after we said "I do," chronic pain and illness began to dominate our life. As one trial after another has come, and the complexities and weight of prolonged suffering have brought us both to the end of ourselves, our marriage has been tested in more ways than I ever imagined it would be.

Sadly, I know that we aren't alone. Statistically, chronic

illnesses—"those that last a year or more and require ongoing medical attention or that limit activities of daily living" (US Dept. of Health and Human Services, 2010)—affect approximately 133 million Americans, representing more than 40% of the population. The percentage is similar in the UK. That means that a high number of marriages are being impacted by ongoing pain—pain that is often invisible to others. That's a *lot* of couples, and yet we don't tend to talk about it much (and not at all if it's possible to hide it when we're in public or sitting in church). But we need to talk about it, because the pain can be devastating—not only to our bodies and our sense of selves but to our marriages and our faith. Satan knew this:

> All that a man has he will give for his life. But [he said to God] stretch out your hand and touch his bone and his flesh, and he will curse you to your face.
>
> (Job 2 v 4-5)

Inescapable physical pain can create a constant sense of desperation for escape and relief, tainting the sufferer's view of everything and everyone, including their spouse and including God. It's no wonder, then, that Satan would take full advantage of this form of suffering and use it as a weapon against us, our marriages, and our relationship with Christ.

But praise God that he can use the enemy's schemes to advance his own good purposes. Praise God, our marriages can survive, and even strengthen, in the face of this trial. If you or your spouse are one of the many suffering in this way, and you find yourselves trying to navigate marriage through the unique challenges that it has brought, I'd like to encourage you. Although your pain and heartache are very real, you do not need to navigate this road alone. If Christ has not chosen to bring physical healing as of yet, then he promises to equip both you and your spouse with enduring grace and strength for the cross he has entrusted you to carry.

PRAY FOR RELIEF, TRUST IN GRACE FOR TODAY

For the spouse who suffers chronically, there is always a tension between wanting to escape the pain and learning to trust God and rest in where he has you. For the other spouse, the burden is different but also heavy. They carry a great load of responsibility, grieve the loss of how things used to be, and, worst of all, feel helpless and frustrated with their inability to ease their loved one's pain. As each of us grieve the loss of what chronic illness has robbed us of, our responses to pain (ours or our loved one's) are not always rational, let alone godly. Personally, when I'm fighting through pain to care for my family, I'm easily irritated and quick to snap at Jeff or the kids over something incredibly minor. On the flip side, when I'm couch-ridden, Jeff can get worn down by the added burdens he has to carry, which can tempt him to give in to resentment, impatience, and frustration. Though Jeff knows that my pain is not my fault, and I know that he desires to love me well in the midst of it, we both struggle not to turn against one another.

This is where a marriage is tested. When we have no guarantee of our circumstances changing, we are faced with the choice of becoming bitter, resentful, and closed-off to one another, or, by God's grace, turning to him in our disappointments and pain—dependent on the grace and strength of Christ to press on and love our spouse with a love beyond ourselves. The choice is yours to make.

Job and his wife faced it too. Job had every reason to turn his back on God and yet chose to trust his sovereignty and the path of humble surrender:

The LORD gave, and the LORD has taken away; blessed be the name of the LORD ... Shall we receive good from God, and shall we not receive evil? (1 v 21; 2 v 10)

Job's wife, however, struggled to join her husband in such a response. "Curse God and die," she told him (2 v 9). And, in many ways, I can empathize with her. She too had just lost her children, her wealth and her security, and now she was helplessly watching as her once confident, strong, respected husband sat covered in ashes and moaning in agony. Maybe you can begin to sense her fear and helplessness. Maybe you can empathize with her feeling that bitterness was the only option, and that escape was the best outcome.

Job's response appears harsh and blunt, but I think Job is being gracious when he says, "You speak as one of the foolish women would speak. Shall we receive good from God, and shall we not receive evil?" (2 v 10). He does not call her a foolish woman, but rather characterizes her as someone speaking *like* a foolish woman. He challenges her wrong thinking rather than excusing it, but at the same time he doesn't attack her character. *You're not acting as the woman I know you to be,* he says.

What we say and how we say it makes all the difference in these moments. Pain will inevitably bring our sin and our spouse's sin to the surface. When it does, we should neither ignore it by sweeping it under the rug nor attack our spouse for struggling. We need to respond with empathy and understanding to our spouse's pain, while gently and graciously pointing them to the truth in love. That is hard.

And we need to be willing to listen to truth, too—in the pages of Scripture and from the lips of our husband or wife. When we are in pain, or when we are watching our spouse suffer with pain, that is hard, too. But it is a choice you have. We don't know how Job's wife chose to respond.

Challenge wrong thinking rather than excusing it, but at the same time don't attack your spouse's character.

Though we know that Job never understood the reason for his suffering and yet was a changed man because of it, we never hear much of Job's wife after her response here. I hope that Job's faith won her to a deeper faith of her own.

HARD DAYS ARE NOT HOPELESS DAYS

Whether you are the suffering spouse, as Job was, or suffering alongside of your spouse, as Dr. McQuilkin was, you can glean wisdom from their godly responses as you walk the hard road of chronic illness in your marriage—not simply to survive, but to experience a deeper love for the Lord and each other in the process.

Should we pray for and seek healing and relief? Yes! It's important that we don't hopelessly resign ourselves to our circumstances as though nothing can or will ever change. But it's equally important that we don't pray only for healing, but also for spiritual sustaining as we wait. We need to ask Jesus to give us the grace to walk steadfastly and joyfully, for the strength to love each other well as we walk, and for the faith to look forward expectantly to a life without pain.

By God's grace, the grievous losses and painful trials that chronic illness has brought to our marriage have not had the final word. Instead, it has been a way by which God has given us a deeper and more satisfying love for one another as we lean into Christ and experience the overflow of his undeserved love. We've enjoyed a richness in our marriage that I'm not sure we would have had if it had not been for the pain we have experienced. I praise God that he loves us enough to take what he must in order to give us what he knows we need. Our days can be very hard, but they are never hopeless and they will not be wasted.

And one day, my body will be free from pain, Jeff's struggle to love me through it will be no more, and we will both marvel in the goodness and faithfulness of Jesus to sustain us until the end:

> *So we do not lose heart. Though our outer self is wasting away, our inner self is being renewed day by day. For this light momentary affliction is preparing for us an eternal weight of glory beyond all comparison, as we look not to the things that are seen but to the things that are unseen. For the things that are seen are transient, but the things that are unseen are eternal. (2 Corinthians 4 v 16-18)*

Until we reach that "eternal weight of glory beyond all comparison," though, it seems that I am going to live with some level of pain for the rest of my earthly life. So I need to learn to pray, "Lord, please, please heal me if it would be your will—but, if it is not, please help me to trust your purposes, and help me love Jeff as you have loved me. Guard me from the deadening cloud of guilt over the burden that I feel like I am, and help me trust that you will give Jeff the strength and endurance for this road that you have called him to walk with me." Maybe you need to pray this way too.

And so it also seems that it means Jeff will need to love and serve a wife who is in pain every day of the rest of our marriage. And I'm praying that he's praying what Dr. McQuilkin prayed: "Lord, I pray you will do a physical miracle in my wife, but if you choose not to, then work a spiritual miracle in me so that I can love her well until the end." Maybe you need to pray this way too.

REFLECT

- If you suffer with chronic illness or pain, how is it affecting your relationship with God (perhaps positively, perhaps negatively)? Will you come to Christ daily, asking not only for healing but for his presence, strength, and peace as you wait on him?
- If your spouse suffers from chronic illness or pain, do you feel resentful toward him/her for the effect their pain has on your life and your marriage? How might God be using their illness as a means of growing and changing both of you to reflect Christ? How can you practically show your spouse that you love them and see them as a gift from God rather than a burden?
- (Together, if possible) Discuss the unique challenges you face, and what has been helpful (and what hasn't been) as you navigate chronic illness together. Are there any changes that you need to make to improve communication and guard against isolating yourselves from one another?
- Discuss all the ways that you have seen God's faithfulness in the past (where he's guided you, how he's changed you, how he's helped you endure when you didn't think you could, and so on).

PRAY

If you are struggling with long-term illness, you could use my prayer from the previous page:

Lord, please, please heal me if it would be your will—but, if it is not, please help me to trust your purposes, and help me love my spouse as you have loved me. Guard me from the deadening cloud of guilt over the burden that I feel like I am, and help me trust that you will give my spouse the strength and endurance for this road that you have called him to walk with me. Amen.

If you are loving and serving someone with chronic illness, pray like Dr. McQuilkin:

Lord, I pray you will do a physical miracle in my wife/husband, but if you choose not to, then work a spiritual miracle in me so that I can love her/him well until the end. Amen.

For further meditation: Psalm 23; Joel 2 v 25-27; 1 Corinthians 13 v 4-7; Ephesians 3 v 16-19.

Journaling

_____

_____

_____

_____

_____

_____

_____

_____

_____

_____

_____

_____

_____

_____

_____

_____

_____

_____

_____

_____

_____

CHAPTER 6

Learning to Lead
(A Word for Husbands)

*Have you considered my servant Job, that there
is none like him on the earth, a blameless and
upright man, who fears God and turns away
from evil? (Job 1 v 8b)*

*"Lord, how do I lead my family when I feel so weak?
I'm sinking under the burdens and can't seem to catch
my breath. I feel helpless in the face of overwhelming
circumstances which I carry with no end in sight. Help
me to trust your infinite wisdom and knowledge, and
to be obedient to where you are calling me and my
family. Help me lead my family well, using the time
and resources you have entrusted to me: to love my wife
despite the struggles that have come between us and to
be the dad my kids need, when these things feel beyond
my own wisdom and strength.*

*"Whatever it takes, Lord, I choose to delight in and
depend on you. I am weak, but you are strong.
Glorify your name through all of this brokenness
and pain."*

A few years ago, I wrote this prayer during an intense season of trials in our family. I was on call 24/7 as a trauma surgery consultant, often having to choose between my responsibility at work and being with Sarah in moments when she needed me most. Some days, watching my wife and children suffer, and sensing that I was failing them, felt too much to bear. I wondered how much longer we—I—could endure. Our son's challenges had increased, our family was battling Lyme Disease, our bank account was drained by medical bills, and I felt stuck in a job that only contributed to the stress in our home. Our marriage was suffering, and distance and resentment was building between us.

I recognized my role as the leader of the home, but I was barely staying afloat myself. How could I lead anyone else?

I was sinking, and I was praying—and by God's grace he answered, and continues to answer.

I have learned that being a leader doesn't mean I have to have it all together or feel in control at all times. Instead, I have to remember that God equips those he calls, and that he builds us up as we spend time in his word and prayer daily, learning to look to him in humility and dependence, not shirking our responsibility in a selfish desire for ease nor abusing it in a distorted attempt to control.

We see this kind of husband and father in Job, who led his family by living an upright and blameless life, fearing God and turning away from evil. Was he perfect? No. But his life was marked by pursuing godliness in and out of his home. His faith overflowed into the care he showed for his family, as he continually prayed for his children even after they'd grown up.

You may feel a long, long way away from Job—not so much in his suffering, but in his response to suffering and in the kinds of ways he cared for his family and clung to his faith. If you do, you're not alone; and, strangely, you're in a good place. Admitting to Christ our weakness and inability is the best place for us to start. We can, by God's grace and with his help, make progress in being the men our families would like us to be and need us to be.

SACRIFICE, NOT SUPERIORITY

First we need to understand the high calling we've been given as husbands, and we do that as we look not to our own marriages but to Christ's marriage to his chosen people, the church. That is the model that our marriages are designed to reflect. The theologian and historian Geoffrey Bromiley described it this way: "As God made man in his own image, so he made earthly marriage in the image of his own eternal marriage with his people" (*God and Marriage*, page 43). And so "the husband is the head of the wife even as [that is, in the same way that] Christ is the head of the church, his body" (Ephesians 5 v 23). Your marriage is designed to mirror and point to the nature of the relationship between Jesus and his people.

So this "headship" that we are called to is not about superiority—it's about sacrifice:

> *Husbands, love your wives, as Christ loved the church*
> *and gave himself up for her, that he might sanctify*
> *her, having cleansed her by the washing of water*
> *with the word, so that he might present the church*
> *to himself in splendor, without spot or wrinkle or*
> *any such thing, that she might be holy and without*
> *blemish. (Ephesians 5 v 25-27)*

Christ's life on earth gives us a blueprint for our marriage relationship. We lead as we love, and we must love "as Christ loved the church and gave himself up for her" (v 25):

In the same way husbands should love their wives
as their own bodies. He who loves his wife loves
himself. For no one ever hated his own flesh, but
nourishes and cherishes it, just as Christ does the
church, because we are members of his body.

(v 28-30)

When Christ came to earth, he didn't lead his followers by abusing his power for personal gain, or by shaming or coercing them into following him. Yes, he led with strength, truth, and authority, but he was also characterized by gentleness, compassion, and sacrificial love. As husbands, we are called to follow Christ's example, leading by serving, loving by caring, doing what we can to make our home one where our bride feels protected and where Christ-likeness is celebrated.

The theologian Joel R. Beeke describes it this way:

"Sacrifice for her. Provide for her and cherish her just
as you love your own body. Give her your thoughts,
your time, your talk, your tenderness, and your
touch—but make sure you touch her heart before
you touch her body. Stop measuring out your love in
small spoonfuls according to what she has done for
you lately. Start pouring out your love by the bucket
according to the infinite riches of Christ's love for you
… The most important gift you can give your wife is
not money, a house, a car, jewelry, or even yourself.
The best gift you can give her is to bring her to God
so that she can glorify Him and enjoy Him forever. So
speak the Word of God to her. Pray for her soul."
(How Should Men Lead Their Families? page 14)

Brothers, we mustn't pass over this aspect of our leadership too quickly. Too often, marriage advice stops at exhorting men to take leadership in the home, but it fails to flesh out how we are to do so with a heart that nourishes, cherishes, and adores our wives.

- To *nourish* your wife means you are her provider: not only for her material needs, but for her physical, emotional, and spiritual nourishment. We do a disservice to our wives when we assume that what she needs most from us is to bring home a paycheck, play with the kids, and pursue her physically. Nourishing her requires a sacrificial attention to and investment in the marriage. Encourage your wife and seek to know her heart—her interests, fears, insecurities, goals, strengths, and weaknesses. The goal of nourishing your marriage is to see it grow, develop, and mature, so that it provides a clearer and clearer picture of Christ's marriage with the church. So we must be willing to invest ourselves wholeheartedly in the woman we married.

- When you *cherish* your wife, you see her as a daughter of your heavenly Father. She is a precious gift, not to be misused, ignored, or taken advantage of. You are to build her up in Christ, displaying a tender, genuine care and protection of her. Look at your wife as Adam looked at Eve—the only woman on earth for you. There is no other woman that should capture your heart like your wife. If you struggle to feel that way in the moment, ask God to give you the eyes to see her as he does. When you cherish her, your heart finds enjoyment in your wife's joy and pleasure more than in your own.

- Lastly, to *adore* your wife is to see her as beautiful, inside and out. It is to dwell on what is best about her; to celebrate the ways she is like Christ, and to encourage her to become more and more like him; to see her as Christ does, and to lead her to see herself as Christ does as well.

This often doesn't come naturally, especially when tension, distrust, or hurt has already taken root within our marriage, or when trials are buffeting us. You may feel far from being able to step up and fulfill such a high calling; maybe you currently lack any real desire to do so, or you're battling physical or mental weakness. But none of us are left to our own resources and strength. Part of the fruit of the Spirit, when it grows in the heart of a husband, is this kind of headship. And so it's the Spirit's work, and we can (and must) pray for it and pursue it and trust him to grow us in it. We can ask Jesus, through his Spirit, to give us his love for our bride and the strength to step up to our God-given role. We can ask him to open our eyes to sin, areas of weakness, and challenges that are hindering our leadership.

Brother, there are only two things stopping you and me from being the husbands that Christ calls us to be and that our wives need us to be—your sin, and her sin. A husband's sin can cause him to shrink from leadership through fear or laziness, or to be harsh in leadership through pride or selfishness. And our wives are sinful—saved and beautiful, but sinful—and that can cause loving headship to be hard work, particularly if it's not the established pattern of the relationship thus far. But still we're called to do it; still we must do it—not perfectly, but deliberately and prayerfully.

STEP UP IN HIS STRENGTH

Wives, if you're reading this, your encouragement and support is more valuable than you know. Many of us husbands feel the weight and great responsibility of our call as the head of our family more than we often verbalize. As we struggle to be a godly husband, and as we often fall short of the man and husband we desire to be, any time, space, encouragement, and grace you give us to grow in leading you well is hugely appreciated. Above all else, please notice, celebrate, and pray for Christ-likeness in us.

Men, as leaders who follow the Leader who carried a cross, we are to be more concerned about the wellbeing and heart of our wife than our own life and comfort. The wonderful truth is that just as Christ laid down his life for the joy that was set before him (Hebrews 12 v 2), we will experience joy and satisfaction in walking in God's commands, as we lead, love, nourish, cherish, and adore our wives in such a way that it makes it easy for them to follow our lead.

There will be times when you feel far from this. No marriage is perfect. It's rarely easy to lead. If that's where you find yourself right now, turn to Christ and ask for his strength to take the next step. Perfection will not be achieved on this side of heaven—and that's ok. We can paralyze ourselves by dwelling on what feels unachievable, but if we rely on Jesus, he promises to enable us for what he has called us to. Rather than being demoralized by how you're never going to be like Jesus, or giving up because you're never going to be like Jesus, simply seek to be a more Christ-like husband today than you were yesterday.

There is incredible joy in laying down your life for the woman that God has entrusted to you for a time. What a privilege and great responsibility you have been given to love and care for a daughter of the King. Nourish her. Cherish her. Adore her. Show her you will fight for her no matter the cost. Love her well by loving Christ more.

REFLECT

- How does understanding that your role as a husband is to sacrificially love and lead your wife, as Christ does the church, encourage, convict, or challenge you?
- If you feel overwhelmed by what the Bible calls husbands to be (and even if you don't!)… what is one area in your marriage that you will ask God to grow you in this week? What would progress in loving headship in that area look like?
- What are some ways you would like to grow in nourishing, cherishing, and adoring your wife?
- (Together, if possible) Ask your wife to tell you three ways in which you are loving her sacrificially; and two ways in which she would like you to pray and work to love her better.
- Wives: Encourage your husband in ways that show you appreciate his leadership (even if they seem small), and share with him ways that you feel (or would like to feel) nourished, cherished, and adored. Ask him how you can support and pray for his leadership.

PRAY

Heavenly Father, thank you for your Son's perfect example of what sacrificial leadership looks like. By your grace, Lord, humble me and mold me into the godly man and husband you have created me to be. Lord, show me how to love in a way that builds my wife up, and that brings glory to you. Help our marriage to reflect Christ more. Lord, you know the ways I struggle to love my wife sacrificially—and Lord, please show me the failings that I have not yet noticed. Forgive me for not always loving and leading your daughter well. Thank you that your mercies to me, and to her, are new every day—give me a heart that is

*fixed on you and able to reflect more of you today than
I did yesterday. I choose to trust you, Lord, and I pray
that what you have allowed in our marriage will now
be used greatly for your purposes. Amen.*

For further meditation: 1 Corinthians 11 v 1-3; 1 Corinthians 16 v 13-14; Ephesians 5 v 25-33.

Journaling

CHAPTER 7

Learning to Follow
(A Word for Wives)

Then his wife said to him, "Do you still hold fast
your integrity? Curse God and die." (Job 2 v 9)

The fact that I am writing a chapter on submission is both humorous and precious to me. I've never been one to enjoy taking instruction. If you told me to go right, I'd go left. If I was told to be quiet, suddenly I had much to say. Although God has used my strong will for his good purposes, my stubborn spirit has also taken me down quite a few painful paths in my lifetime. My resistance to the idea of submitting was only further strengthened through experiences of being hurt during times of vulnerability. No, submission isn't something that has ever come naturally to me.

RESCUING SUBMISSION

The problem with the word "submission" is that our minds and hearts naturally jump to "marriage," when really they should jump to "discipleship." Submission should make us think not so much about being a wife as simply being a Christian. Submission is the basic posture of a Christian, and it's good and joyful and positive because ultimately we are submitting to the perfect Lord Jesus. He promises us:

Come to me, all who labor and are heavy laden, and I will give you rest. Take my yoke upon you, and learn from me, for I am gentle and lowly in heart, and you will find rest for your souls. For my yoke is easy, and my burden is light. (Matthew 11 v 28-30)

As we submit to Christ and trust his direction, we receive his yoke—his teaching, character, and leading—and find rest for our souls. Submitting to Christ as Lord is not only a command but the way to freedom and rest. It's no surprise, then, that it's also an area that Satan has worked hard to distort and undermine since the beginning of time. Author P.B. Wilson wrote, "There are few areas in life that Satan has not attempted to pervert, but submission to authority has always been high on his list of priorities" (*Liberated Through Submission*, page 102).

We'll never understand or accept the idea of a wife submitting to her husband unless we first grasp that submission in marriage is meant to reflect that greater submission to Christ:

Wives, submit to your own husbands, as to the Lord. For the husband is the head of the wife even as Christ is the head of the church, his body, and is himself its Savior. Now as the church submits to Christ, so also wives should submit in everything to their husbands.
(Ephesians 5 v 22-24)

You may have witnessed a wonderful example of biblical submission and, despite the bad press the word has been given, you have seen the blessing of living out God's design. If that is true of you, see that as a great gift!

But for many others, you question how any blessing can come through the act of submission. It may simply be that the idea of submission sounds outdated. But it may be that the word makes the hairs on the back of your neck stand up or your blood begin to boil, because you've experienced or watched abusive or domineering leadership that twisted the Bible's commands to excuse what was in fact sin. Perhaps your experience tells you that submission means being treated as inferior, feeling unloved, and being silenced and taken advantage of.

If that is you, I'm so very sorry. I hurt for you and the harmful distortions that you've experienced, especially when evil has been condoned or excused. Please hear me: this type of "leadership" is not biblical and goes against the very heart of God; and he promises that all will one day be held accountable. But don't run from biblical submission because you've been deeply hurt by unbiblical abuse.

So what is submission for a wife to her husband? We need to understand how each of God's commands to submit are rooted and anchored in our submission to the Lord (a command given to both the husband and wife), and designed to reflect the gospel.

Just as God the Father, Jesus the Son, and the Holy Spirit are equally God but are distinct and fulfill unique roles, men and women are equally created in the image of God, equally valuable (Genesis 1 v 26-28), yet each created to uniquely display different facets of our Creator. To say that the husband is greater (of more worth or value) than the wife would be like saying the Father is greater than the Son, which goes against all of Scripture (for instance, John 5 v 21-23). It's in that context that we must read God's word to husbands and wives in Ephesians 5.

Though this truth may sound oppressive to those looking through our culture's distorted lens, when the roles of husband and wife are lived out biblically, it's not only life-giving in a marriage but also a beautiful reflection of the gospel. I find Christina Fox's description incredibly helpful:

"The unique roles that men and women have in marriage serve as a living message of the gospel. The husband models the love that Jesus portrayed in laying down his life for the church. And a wife then models the church's submission to her Bridegroom— the church's trust and respect … The church follows Jesus as her head and uses her gifts to carry out his mission in this world. Likewise, the wife respects and yields to her husband's leadership as she uses her gifts to complement his good purposes for their marriage and family." (Designed for Joy, pages 69-70)

A woman's call to submission is a far cry from being treated as a doormat. Rather, it's a call to be a strong, wise, fearless woman of faith who is adorned with a quiet confidence—not to rule over her husband but to honor and help him fulfill the high calling of leading in a way that reflects Christ. It is neither an imposition of equality or servitude but a celebration of difference. Submission doesn't devalue women; in fact, it shows just how valuable we are in God's eyes. It's as if he says to our husband, "Son, love my daughter by laying your life down for her as I have for you. Protect, serve, care for, and lead her in a way that enables her to reflect more of me. That's how precious she is to me." And he says to us as wives, "Daughter, use your gifts and strengths to support, encourage, and honor your husband in a way that helps him live out his weighty responsibility of leading and loving you well."

WHEN MARRIAGES FALL FAR SHORT

God's purpose for marriage is to display the gospel and bring him glory, in a husband's loving headship and a wife's loving submission. But it is important to acknowledge that many marriages fall far short of God's design.

If you are suffering in your marriage because of abuse, or an addiction such as pornography, please reach out to a pastor or other godly leader for counsel. If you are not safe in your marriage, remove yourself (and any children) and get help. While God can redeem and heal even seemingly hopeless relationships, he never asks us to submit to an abusive or harmful situation, or to walk through it alone. If your husband ever asks you to sin, treats you in a harmful way, or "leads" by inducing fear, you are loving him, and your Lord, by refusing to submit to sin and by refusing to treat it as normal or acceptable.

AN ENCOURAGING FOLLOWER

For most of us, however, the challenge to follow our husband's leadership stems not from his sin but from our own desire for control. These struggles only increase when outside pressures and trials begin to press in.

We see this in the unbelieving response of Job's wife in Job 2 v 9, as she struggled to follow Job's godly leadership during a pivotal (and deeply painful) moment in their lives: "Do you still hold fast your integrity?" she challenges him: "Curse God and die." Here was a woman who was struggling, and failing, to submit to God and the devastating circumstances that he had allowed. And, out of her lack of trust in and submission to the Lord, she then sought to lead her husband to curse the Almighty.

Of course, you likely don't encourage your husband to curse God, but how easy it is to seek to lead and resist the call to submit when life is hard or when our husband does not do what we think he should. When our lives are flipped upside down—we're diagnosed with a life-altering illness, we're struggling to have children, our husband loses his job, and so on—our response to disappointment and our desire for control can illuminate struggles that we've never recognized within our hearts and marriage. Fear of where we're heading, grief over what we've lost, and unbelief can motivate us not only to respond in unbelief but to step over our husband's leadership (or lack of it) and take control in whatever way we can.

These are the moments to remember that submitting is a part of our discipleship, that we can please God as we follow our husband, that submission isn't submission if it's contingent on us agreeing with our husband's decisions, and that every time we choose to sacrifice our own desires in order to follow (unless we're being led into sin or harm), we are strengthening our marriage.

However, at the same time, we are also to use the wisdom and discernment that God has given us to encourage and work alongside our husband in making life's decisions—and to courageously and respectfully push against anything that dishonors the Lord. As Eric Schumacher and Elise Fitzpatrick point out from the courageous account of Abigail in 1 Samuel 25 (who took action, without her husband's permission or knowledge, for the sake of righteousness):

> *"Though Christian wives are called to submit to their husband's godly leadership, that doesn't mean that they should stand quietly by and do nothing while their husband foolishly brings destruction on himself and others." (Worthy, page 131)*

It is good and right to submit to godly (though imperfect) leadership and encourage our husband in it. It is equally good and right to bravely stand up against what is ungodly for the sake of honoring Christ.

OK, SO WHAT DOES THIS LOOK LIKE?

Though it will look slightly different for each of us in its outward expression, honoring our husband should be reflected in our thoughts, words, and actions, and motivated by the "gentle and quiet spirit" that Peter writes about in his first letter:

> *Let your adorning be the hidden person of the heart*
> *with the imperishable beauty of a gentle and quiet*
> *spirit, which in God's sight is very precious.*
>
> *(1 Peter 3 v 4)*

A gentle spirit is one that reflects meekness and humility—not weakness or inferiority. It begins with the disposition of our hearts and is reflected through an attitude of quiet strength and peace in the ways we speak and act toward our husbands. It's the opposite of being manipulative, demanding, or driven by fear.

Similarly, a quiet spirit is not referring to the volume or amount of words spoken, because we can and should be an equal partner in all areas of the relationship, but it means to be settled and steadfast, and slow to criticism and harshness. As we live this way, we will not only be personally blessed with peace and freedom, but it will be life-giving in our relationship with our husband.

When we come with humility and quiet confidence to our conversations, disagreements, and the challenges we face as a couple, it will help our husbands to hear our feelings and our counsel and enable us together to work through it as a united partnership. And we will be less inclined to talk over or belittle our husbands when they express a different opinion. It will enable us to use our gifts and strengths, while still honoring and helping them to live out their call to lead, serve, and love sacrificially.

In the end, there's no how-to manual for submission within marriage. Rather, it's about prayerfully seeking to live according to God's design as you work through decisions and preferences in love and respect, while honoring

In the harder parts
of your marriage,
you have a great
opportunity to put the
gospel on display.

your commitment to each other and to the roles God has laid out for each of you. Your husband is a sinner, and he won't always get it right. Don't demand perfection, or use his failings as an excuse not to walk in obedience to the Lord. Instead, affirm him when he does lead lovingly, and gently encourage him to step up and lead when he's tempted not to.

PUTTING THE GOSPEL ON DISPLAY

I do wonder how different things could have been for Job and his wife had she submitted to the Lord and brought her grief, sorrow, and pain to him in faith; and then encouraged her husband to lead her in her struggles, instead of challenging him to follow her down the path of faithlessness. Instead of it being a moment of division, it could have been an opportunity for her to honor God by following Job's lead. What a powerful moment it could have been for them to stand firmly together and experience the blessing of walking side by side in faith, through their grief.

If your marriage is like mine, there will be areas where you find it easier to submit, and areas where you find it hard and costly. In those harder parts, you have a choice in how you will respond and a great opportunity to put the gospel on display in how you treat your husband (whether he "deserves" it or not). By God's grace, may God empower us to honor, respect, and support our husbands as the men God has called to lead and love us—for the joy of our marriages and for the glorious purpose of reflecting Christ and his church.

REFLECT

- Has your understanding of submission been different than what we've seen in God's word in this chapter? In what ways? Have you been taught that a "gentle and quiet spirit" means you don't have an equal voice or value within the marriage? If so, how has this chapter challenged that view and encouraged you to see that though a husband and wife have different roles, they have an equal value and voice as they use their God-given gifts, strengths, and responsibilities in a way that honors Christ and blesses the relationship?

- In what ways do you struggle to submit to what God has allowed? What fear or unbelief is keeping you from trusting God's control over your life? What would a spirit of trust-filled submission look like?

- Wives, are there any areas that the Holy Spirit has brought to mind where you struggle to honor and respect your husband (in thoughts, words, or actions)? Will you ask God to give you both the desire and ability to honor, support, and help your husband live out his call to godly leadership?

- Husbands, do you see any way that you have wrongly viewed or used these verses on submission as an excuse for control and selfish gain? Do you live with your wife in a way that values and encourages her to voice her thoughts, opinions, and wisdom?

- (Together, if possible) Discuss what thoughts and feelings arise when you think of submission, and what ways your past or upbringing has negatively or positively impacted your view of biblical submission (both to Christ's lordship and within a marriage). Discuss where submission to the Lord has been difficult and where you want to grow in trusting and obeying him more.

PRAY

Lord, I confess that I often struggle to submit to your plan for me, including your design for marriage. I struggle to let go of control and I find it hard to trust that what you allow in my life is truly for my eternal good. Help me to grow in a spirit of humility and faith, to wholeheartedly submit to you as Lord, and to believe that your plan for me is good—even when it doesn't feel like it. Jesus, in a world that tells us to be independent and strong, it's hard to see submission in marriage as a blessing. Please reshape my view of what godly submission is and open my eyes to the goodness and beauty of honoring and submitting to my husband, despite the resistance I sometimes feel within me. Make me a woman who fears, honors, and trusts you above all else, and grow in me a gentle and quiet spirit that honors my husband and glorifies you. Amen.

For further meditation: Romans 13 v 1-7; James 4 v 7; 1 Peter 3 v 5-6.

Journaling

_____

_____

_____

_____

_____

_____

_____

_____

_____

_____

_____

_____

_____

_____

_____

_____

_____

_____

_____

_____

_____

CHAPTER 8

Only God Can Change a Heart: When Your Spouse Fails You

My breath is strange to my wife; and I am a stench
to the children of my own mother. (Job 19 v 17)

He'll *never understand how I really feel. He wasn't there for me when I needed him most, so how can I trust him when he can't see how deeply I've been hurt.*

After days of heated conversations, tears, and unresolved hurts boiling over, I wondered if there was any way forward. On one hand, it was a miracle that we were still together after all we had been through: my chronic illness, Jeff being on call 24/7 for nine years, a child with special needs, four children with Lyme Disease, job loss, financial loss, several major surgeries, and intimacy struggles... And yet, on the other hand, we had been in survival mode for so long that neither of us had had the time or energy to face what was brewing under the surface. With significant challenges demanding our constant attention, the seemingly less urgent things, those hurts and disagreements, continued to go by the wayside.

Then we found ourselves in a brief season of slight reprieve, and those "lesser" things began to demand attention. Feelings that I hadn't even realized I was carrying started brewing in me. Anger, resentment, hurt, and trust issues began to erupt as though an emotional volcano had been simmering below the surface for years too long.

For the first time in our marriage, we began to understand how easily couples reach a breaking point from which escape seems to be the only answer. Though we never verbalized or acted on these thoughts, I know they were there.

I attempted to share with Jeff how the layers of hurt and the painful experiences that I had walked through day after day had left deep scars. How desperately I longed for Jeff to see, understand, and tend to my hurting heart. Yet every time I attempted to describe my pain and what I thought he needed to hear, trying to articulate my feelings in ways he could understand, I only walked away more discouraged and angry. It seemed clear to me that he needed to change for us to move forward; and if I could help him see where he needed to change, we would be on a path to healing.

I don't know how long it took for me to realize the futility of my attempts to convince him to "see me" in the way I thought I needed him to. There came a point, though, when the Lord began to show me that though my desire for healing wasn't wrong, my focus on Jeff as the sole problem was. While I was trying to open my husband's eyes, the Lord was opening my own. After weeks of exhausting conversations and tension between the two of us, I increasingly brought my heartache and frustrations to the Lord. I stopped pleading with Jeff, and I started pleading with the Lord.

> "Lord, help me take my eyes off of my husband and
> what I think I need from him, and trust my hurts,
> fears, and desires to you. I know from Psalm 139
> that you are the only one who sees and knows me

completely, and you alone can satisfy my deepest longings. Please help me see my own sin and not elevate his above my own. Give me a greater understanding of the mercy and forgiveness that you have shown me and, in your strength, help me to entrust Jeff and our marriage to you. If it's best, open his eyes to see the ways I have felt hurt, and give me the humility to see how I have wronged him. Only you can rebuild our marriage on a foundation of love and trust in you as our Savior. Please take this brokenness—my brokenness—and build something wonderful and lasting. But, Lord, even if we never move past this point, help me to love Jeff out of an overflow of your love for me. I can't do this in my own strength."

As I began to pray and spend more time in God's word every day, I felt a burden begin to lift off my shoulders. Instead of trying to come up with new ways to make my points to Jeff, I started to share with him how God was growing me—including confessing to Jeff ways that I had wronged him, but had been too blind to see. Instead of trying to convince Jeff that he needed to change, I trusted God to do the changing work as he saw fit.

Though we still had many hard, honest conversations to navigate, they became more fruitful. Amazingly (but not surprisingly), when we stopped trying to change each other and started asking Christ to change our own hearts, God began to do a deeper work in each of us, and a wonderful work of healing began in our marriage. That season of struggle for us has now become a marker of God's faithfulness.

Although circumstances will vary, many marriages experience similar struggles, which are likely magnified for those who have endured more extreme suffering. Sometimes they come when the storm is at its fiercest, but oftentimes they hit when the storm itself has blown out and left some wreckage to sort out in its aftermath.

Let's be realistic—two sinners living under the same roof are bound to hurt, sin against, and misunderstand one another—a lot. Added to that, we each have unique temperaments, different past influences and degrees of spiritual maturity, and distinctively male or female lenses—all of which make things even more interesting.

I don't think we're the only couple who know what Job was trying to express when he said, "My breath is strange to my wife; and I am a stench to the children of my own mother" (Job 19 v 17). Their suffering (and their different responses to it) created distance between them. For whatever reason—whether it was that she resented his continued trust in the Lord or that his illness made him physically repulsive—he was acutely aware of the distance between them.

How do we prevent things reaching that point? Or, if they have already done so, what does it take to move forward?

THE ONE PERSON YOU NEED IS NOT YOUR SPOUSE

If we get this backwards, then our pursuit of joy and our desire to be known and unconditionally loved will be primarily directed at each other, setting our marriages up for frustration, disappointment, and hurt when our "needs" and desires fail to be met. You will actually enjoy your spouse more when you're not looking to them to be everything you need, or demanding they change to become who you want them to be and then resenting them when they don't or can't—or even won't (if they are not a Christian or if, for the time being, they're unwilling to consider the state of their own heart).

The truth is, there will always be something that you desire to change about your spouse (from small annoyances to damaging sinful choices), and there will always be things that they desire to change about you. But when you look to Christ to satisfy your desires, you will place fewer unrealistic expectations on each other and enjoy one another more freely.

THE PERSON WHO MOST NEEDS TO CHANGE MAY NOT BE YOUR SPOUSE

How easy it is to read Jesus' warnings against double standards and think of other people who need to hear it—and how ironic it is that we so often do this. But when Jesus asks, "Why do you see the speck that is in your brother's eye, but do not notice the log that is in your own eye?" (Matthew 7 v 13), he is talking to me—and, likely, you. We are all prone to downplay our own actions and motives while condemning the actions of others and assuming the worst about their motives. It's no different in marriage. We tend to fixate on our spouse's shortcomings while excusing or not even seeing our own.

Paul says a Christian should "not ... think of himself more highly than he ought to think, but [should] think with sober judgment ... according to [his God-given] measure of faith" (Romans 12 v 3). Only when we see ourselves rightly can we "in humility count others more significant than yourselves" (Philippians 2 v 3).

If you are a Christian, your faith tells you that you are a sinner in need of mercy. Living in view of that truth will make you quicker to forgive, and much slower to assume that the problem is your spouse. The answer may not be "yes," but the question always to ask as you look in the mirror is "Am I the main problem here?" Answer that question and your marriage will be more likely to enjoy an atmosphere that promotes growth and unity, rather than dissension and distance.

THE ONLY PERSON YOU CAN CHANGE IS YOU

Whether your spouse is a Christ-follower or not, you have neither the job of changing them nor the ability to do so. But God can, and will, change *you*. So you can "work out your own salvation with fear and trembling, for it is God who works in you, both to will and to work for his good pleasure" (Philippians 2 v 12-13). Galatians 5 v 25 calls this keeping in step with the Spirit.

God calls us to walk in holiness, and he empowers us to do so through his Spirit.

You cannot change your spouse. So if you desire change or growth in your marriage, it always has to begin with you. Take your eyes off of your spouse and their flaws, and humbly ask the Lord to show you where you need to change, and to work in you by his Spirit so that you can change.

THE ONLY PERSON WHO CAN CHANGE YOUR SPOUSE IS GOD

If God can change you, he can change your spouse! He alone has the power and wisdom to convict, grow, and shape their heart to reflect more of his. So, ask him to do those things—ask him to change your spouse if and where he sees best. Rather than challenging them, growing frustrated, and nagging, we can pray! It is hard to be angry with someone we are praying for. It is easier to love someone we have asked God to be at work in. Next time the temperature is rising and you are about to snap at the person you married, stop. Pray.

And then be patient. Often there are no quick fixes, either for our own heart or our spouse's. God's timetable and ways are not our own, and it is often through long seasons of waiting that he chooses to work. Jeff and I walked through 13 years of marriage before God suddenly moved and changed both of us within a matter of months. Was that long season difficult? Immensely. But I believe those years were preparing us for the work God had purposed to do in each one of us. And for that, I am thankful.

If you've been humbling yourself, praying, waiting, and hoping for change that seems like it may never come, don't lose hope. It's not your job to change anyone else—it is your task to love them. As we will discuss in a later chapter, seasons of waiting are never pointless, and there is always more going on than we are able to see in the moment. Keep asking for the change to come. And you never know—God might just change your own heart in the process.

REFLECT

- What feelings toward your spouse are you harboring and keeping silent about that are harming your intimacy (spiritual, emotional, physical)? Are there ways in which you are elevating your spouse's faults and sins but ignoring your own? Is there anything you need to ask forgiveness for—from God and from your spouse?

- Do you ever treat your spouse in a way that tells them that they are the problem and that if they would change, everything would be better? What would be different if you worked to change yourself with God's help, and focused on their needs rather than their failings? What is one thing you will do for your spouse today that is selfless and expects nothing in return from them, but shows them you care?

- Are there any ways in which you are looking to your spouse too much to meet your needs in a way that they were never meant to be met?
- (Together, if possible) Name three things about your spouse that you want to praise God for and are thankful for in your marriage.

PRAY

Jesus,
Lead me in your truth and teach me,
  for you are the God of my salvation;
  for you I wait all the day long.
Remember your mercy, O LORD, and your steadfast
    love,
  for they have been from of old.
Remember not the sins of my youth or my
    transgressions;
  according to your steadfast love remember me,
  for the sake of your goodness, O LORD!
Good and upright is the LORD;
  therefore he instructs sinners in the way.
He leads the humble in what is right,
  and teaches the humble his way. (Psalm 25 v 5-9)

Help me take my eyes off of my husband/wife and
bring my concerns, fears, and needs to you. Forgive
me for fixating on how I think he/she needs to change
and often ignoring the sin in my own life. Show me
your truth and grow the fruit of your Spirit in me. I
entrust my husband/wife to you and ask for your help
to love them where they are at. Amen.

For further meditation: 1 Corinthians 13 v 4-7; Ephesians 3
v 20 – 4 v 2; Ephesians 4 v 25-31; 1 Peter 4 v 8.

Journaling

_____

_____

_____

_____

_____

_____

_____

_____

_____

_____

_____

_____

_____

_____

_____

_____

_____

_____

_____

_____

_____

_____

_____

CHAPTER 9

When People Bring Judgment Instead of Comfort

*As for me, I would seek God, and to God would I
commit my cause. (Job 5 v 8)*

We sat in the doctor's office, exhausted by the constant struggles with our son, and the doctor said, "I think you just need to give him more to do."

I don't know if he could actually see the steam coming out of my ears and the tears building up, but I couldn't believe that he could look at nine years of turmoil in our home and tell us it was all due to our inability to give our child enough to do.

As hard as comments like that have been, the ones that have hurt the deepest have been from other believers:

"If you discipline him when he acts like that, he won't be so out of control." (Unspoken assumption: You are not good parents.)

"If you just pray and believe in Jesus' name, God will intervene and heal your son." (Unspoken assumption: You don't have enough faith in God.)

"My child struggled exactly like yours, but after we changed his diet and gave him this supplement, everything got better—if you do what we did he'll be fine." (Unspoken assumption: We got it right, you're getting it wrong.)

And it's not just the quick-fix one-liners about the circumstances themselves, but the comments that dismiss or belittle the impact upon our family life.

A hurtful word takes a moment to say and can take a lifetime to recover from. And of course, this can just as easily happen within our marriages. How often Jeff has shared openly about his struggling and hurting, and I have spoken quickly, pointed out where he went wrong or how his thinking is currently wrong, and suggested solutions in ways that make it sound like he is a problem to be fixed—and vice versa when I have shared with him.

In other words: we struggle not to bring judgment instead of comfort.

Why is this? It's hard to sit with another person in the mess of their suffering without trying to impose our own "wisdom" and bring sense to what seems senseless. We want to help. We want to do something. We want it to be better. So we end up, unwittingly, sounding judgmental. More selfishly, we don't like being confronted with the reality that we're not really in control. We don't like rough edges and insurmountable problems. So we're often quick to give pat answers and empty comforts. We input our own experience, not in a humble way that allows it to be ignored if it's unhelpful, but from a position of assuming that we know how someone feels (though we never fully do) or with an assurance that everything will turn out fine (though we never have that guarantee).

We see this clearly in the dialogue recorded between Job and his friends that takes up 33 chapters of the book of Job. At first, the friends wisely offered Job comfort with their silent presence. But as time went on, they could no longer resist pointing out where they thought their friend had gone wrong and suggesting solutions to his suffering.

In Job 5 v 8, Eliphaz responds to Job's wrestling with the

reason for his suffering, "As for me, I would seek God, and to God would I commit my cause." In other words, *If it were me, I would go to God and repent.*

And in Job 8 v 5-7, Bildad presumes, "If you will seek God and plead with the Almighty for mercy, if you are pure and upright, surely then he will rouse himself for you and restore your rightful habitation. And though your beginning was small, your latter days will be very great." In other words, *This is your fault, Job—you must have disobeyed somehow. Make things right with God, and God will bless you with great prosperity.*

Bildad was preaching the same prosperity gospel that we hear all around us today. The truth is, most of us have some degree of the prosperity gospel woven within our thinking: if you do the right thing, you'll be ok, because you can enjoy heaven now. Therefore, you must have done something wrong or not done something required, and that's what has caused your suffering; and/or there must be a way to fix your suffering. If that weren't enough, we often have the desire to be God: to know the reasons, and the answers, and be in control. And so, like Job's friends, we bring judgment instead of comfort, and we offer advice that is unbiblical and unhelpful.

Friend, if you are walking through trials, I have no doubt that you could share how well-intentioned friends have spoken words of comfort that felt more like salt in a wound than salve for the soul. And being on the receiving end of this can quickly cause you to retreat from your church, your friends, and even from your spouse. We swap unhelpful words for unhelpful isolation—and that's no better.

So here are four ways to navigate the difficult waters of not closing yourself off, without exposing yourself to even more hurt.

1. BE GROUNDED IN TRUTH SO YOU CAN RECOGNIZE WHAT IS FALSE

The best way to guard yourself from hurtful and unbiblical comments is to continually fill yourself with the truth and promises of Scripture. Know what God promises and what he does not. Remember that God is never punishing you if your sins have been punished at the cross (Colossians 2 v 13-14). Know that followers of Christ will suffer as we follow our suffering Savior—faith does not insulate us from trials but rather the reverse (1 Peter 2 v 21). We have to be grounded in the word of God, both individually and with our spouse (if they are willing).

2. BEWARE OF ISOLATING YOURSELF OR SEEKING COMMUNITY SOLELY FOR YOUR NEEDS

We have to be careful both not to spend our time listening to the wrong people and equally not to spend our time listening to no one.

Our home life is often exhausting, and mentally and emotionally draining. There have been seasons when we have both been so weary that it's taken every ounce of our physical and emotional energy to show up at our church service, where we know we'll be asked how we are doing. It can be tempting to pull away from the support we actually need.

This happened to me just recently. After days of sinking deeper into despair and retreating from those who care about me, the Holy Spirit gave me the strength to reach out to a select few friends and risk letting them into a very vulnerable area of my life. Though it was hard, it dispelled some of the darkness I was feeling, reminded me that I'm not alone, and gave friends the opportunity and blessing of helping bear my burden alongside of me (Galatians 6 v 2).

Be careful not to
spend time listening
to the wrong people
and equally careful
not to spend your time
listening to no one.

We have to remember that being with the body of Christ is a gift and provision that God has given us, as imperfect and flawed as it is. If we're tempted to believe the lie that "No one understands what I'm going through, and I've been hurt before, so I might as well avoid church and relationships," we are believing a lie of the enemy, who seeks to isolate us from others. As Proverbs 18 v 1 warns us, "Whoever isolates himself seeks his own desire; he breaks out against all sound judgment." As flawed as friends and spouses are, God can and does use these brothers and sisters to gently speak truth into our lives—truths which we don't always want to hear, but often need to hear. Yes, we need friends (and a spouse) who will listen, but we do need them also to speak truth to us too, particularly when our feelings or circumstances are tempting us to believe the lies that God doesn't love us or that he owes us better than this.

We also need to guard against viewing all relationships with a self-serving mindset, falling into the trap of thinking "What can I receive from this person? Will they be able to help me?" We're called not just to allow others to bear our burdens but to bear others' burdens in our turn. God can use what he is doing in our lives—including the hardest parts—to bless and encourage others, often encouraging our own hearts in the process.

3. BE DISCERNING ABOUT WHEN TO PUSH BACK AND WHEN TO LISTEN

Though this is true in any relationship, it can be especially helpful to remember in regards to your marriage. When your spouse shares how they're struggling and is honest about questions that they're wrestling with, be slow to correct them or to fix things for them. Job says to his friends, "Do you think that you can reprove words, when the speech of a despairing man is wind?" (Job 6 v 26). In other words, when we are trying to make sense of our trials and how we feel about them, we may say things that we know aren't biblically true, because our feelings are currently at odds with that truth. Though we know our feelings are not what dictates the truth, we see in Job that God gives us permission to voice our confusion and to honestly wrestle with doubts when what seems to be true is at odds with what God says is true. As John Piper helpfully says:

> "In grief and pain and despair, people often say things they otherwise would not say. They paint reality with darker strokes than they will paint it tomorrow, when the sun comes up. They sing in minor keys, and talk as though that is the only music. They see clouds only, and speak as if there were no sky. What shall we do with these words? Job says that we do not need to reprove them. These words are wind, or literally 'for the wind.' They will be quickly blown away. There will come a turn in circumstances, and the despairing person will waken from the dark night, and regret hasty words."
> (Words for the Wind, www.desiringgod.org)

Don't be that judgmental friend or spouse: simply listen to their struggle, knowing that they are speaking out of their grief rather than their theological belief. Even as you offer gospel truth, you don't need to nitpick over the errors in what they said. The wind has most likely already taken it.

4. BE QUICK TO GIVE GRACE

The irony is that when we're struggling, we can become very judgmental of those who we feel are being judgmental! But as we feel the sting of being given a scorpion when we were needing balm, we can resolve to fight our own tendency to judge and instead respond in grace.

Let's remember that we are all flawed sinners in the process of being made more like Christ. Most people who speak a hurtful comment have good intentions, even when they are unknowingly speaking out of insecurity, fear, or a proud assumption that they "get it." When they do hurt us, we need to remember that there is a good chance that we, too, have unintentionally hurt others at times, and we all need to be quick to extend grace and forgiveness to one another. When we are hurt by the words and judgments of others, as Job was, we need to filter their words through the truth of what God's word says, ask Christ to help us discern what is true and how we need to hear it, and trust that God will ultimately be our defender and our comforter. And as we experience his comfort, by his Spirit, then we are ready to give words of comfort, and not judgment, to those around us who are being tossed by their own storms:

> *Blessed be the ... God of all comfort, who comforts us in all our affliction, so that we may be able to comfort those who are in any affliction, with the comfort with which we ourselves are comforted by God. (2 Corinthians 1 v 3-4)*

REFLECT

- Are you tempted to isolate yourself? If you have isolated yourself, what do you think has caused you to retreat (perhaps past experiences of being hurt, fear, weariness, unbelief)? Can you see challenges and struggles that have increased due to that isolation?
- If you've been hurt, what difference can it make to know that the Lord Jesus knows how that feels? Will you ask him to help you step out in faith, secure in your identity

in him, and let others walk with you through your suffering? What practical step can you take today?

- (Together, if possible) How are you spending your time? Are there areas where you need to cut back so that you can protect the little capacity you have and pour it into what is most important during this season (time in the word, time together as a couple, time in church, relationship with others, and so on)? If so, what steps will you take to implement those changes?

PRAY

Heavenly Father, not only are my trials overwhelming, but the hurtful and ignorant words of others (or sometimes their silence) can make it feel unbearable. Everything in me wants to protect myself and avoid letting others into my pain, yet I know you have created us to be in community with others and to bear each other's burdens. Show me if there are ways in which I need to cut back during this season to use my limited time and energy wisely. Jesus, I need your strength and wisdom to let others in and guard against isolation. In my pride, I struggle to ask for help and, in fear, I worry about what others will think or say. Help me to remember that my suffering is not a sign of your displeasure but is always meant for my good and to draw me nearer to you, even when it exposes my sin. Above all else, thank you that you don't ask me to walk through my suffering alone; thank you that you are always with me. Amen.

For further meditation: Job 42 v 7-11; Ruth 1 – 4; Romans 12 v 15.

Journaling

_____

_____

_____

_____

_____

_____

_____

_____

_____

_____

_____

_____

_____

_____

_____

_____

_____

_____

_____

_____

_____

CHAPTER 10

Waiting Well When God Seems Silent

What is my strength, that I should wait? And what is my end, that I should be patient? (Job 6 v 11)

"Sarah, I just lost my job."

I barely managed to say the words as the realization of what had just happened began to sink in. A complete re-organization had led to nearly all sales employees being laid off, including me. I had four young children and no job.

Less than two years earlier we had been thanking God for that job. After nine years of being on call 24/7 as a trauma consultant, being called into surgeries at any time, day or night, the constant uncertainty and increasing hours were taking its toll on our marriage and family. We took a step of faith, and I left my well-paying industry, trusting that the financial sacrifice would be worth the cost for the sake of our family.

Now here I was, unemployed, struggling with why God had allowed this, and faced with the reality of growing medical bills and the loss of our sole income.

And with that, a season of waiting began.

Sarah and I had waited before—on a house sale, on finding answers to our son's struggles and our other children's health concerns, on healing for Sarah's degenerative ankle. But this felt different to me—it rattled me to the core of my identity. I no longer felt like the provider for our family, and I couldn't escape the reality that our lack of income would soon have drastic consequences for our family.

As I poured myself into finding a new job, I prayed—no, pleaded—for God to intervene.

But the Lord delayed. I had to wait, month after month, with seemingly no end in sight. Many several-month-long interview processes which pointed to promising outcomes all ended with doors being shut in unexpected ways.

Waiting was hard. God's "no"s were confusing when we were in such genuine need. But, looking back, I can now see how it drove me to a deeper dependence on Christ for each step, along with greater confidence in his provision for our family. In time, he provided a new job—and by the time he did, I was a profoundly different person.

JOB'S WAITING

Job had his fair share of waiting too. In a sense, the book of Job is one long wait—for healing, for understanding, for hearing from God, for restoration. And it left him a different person, just as it did me.

Are you in a place of waiting, feeling that your patience and strength, and perhaps your faith, are waning? Are you asking the same questions that Job voiced in Job 6 v 11:

What is my strength, that I should wait? And what is my end, that I should be patient?

Job's suffering is so deep, so profound, that he wonders how he can even go on breathing—and even if he can, what's the point? His perseverance begins to weaken as he loses sight of how and why he should bother. With misery engulfing him and a future that appears bleak, Job doesn't have the strength that would enable him to wait or the hope that would enable him to think there was any point in waiting anyway.

These two questions speak right to the heart of the struggles that we face in our own waiting. If we sense there's no happy ending possible, then why bother? And even if there might be a happy ending, how do we summon up the strength to walk toward it? But, unlike Job, we have the privilege of having all of God's word to help us answer those questions. One particular account in the Bible that gives us profound insight into God's delays and why we can trust him in them is the familiar story of Lazarus:

> *Now a certain man was ill, Lazarus of Bethany, the village of Mary and her sister Martha. It was Mary who anointed the Lord with ointment and wiped his feet with her hair, whose brother Lazarus was ill. So the sisters sent to him, saying, "Lord, he whom you love is ill." But when Jesus heard it he said, "This illness does not lead to death. It is for the glory of God, so that the Son of God may be glorified through it." Now Jesus loved Martha and her sister and Lazarus. So, when he heard that Lazarus was ill, he stayed two days longer in the place where he was.*
> *(John 11 v 1-6)*

When I first read these verses, I thought, "Well that certainly doesn't look like love to me!" But this story gives us the answers to Job's questions (and ours). As we wait, this biblical account offers us three helpful truths.

1. JESUS GLORIFIES HIMSELF THROUGH THE WAITING

God's love doesn't always mean he will give us what we think we need or take away our current pain and heartache.

He loves us by allowing what he must so that we will be ultimately satisfied in him and bring him glory through those circumstances.

> *Now Jesus loved Martha and her sister and Lazarus.*
> *So, when he heard that Lazarus was ill, he stayed*
> *two days longer in the place where he was. (v 5-6)*

Jesus loved them so deeply that he chose to delay. What?! He knew that God would be more glorified by bringing life out of death than removing Lazarus' illness. Here's the thing: Jesus knew that his delay would cause pain to those he loved. Yet he restrained himself from bringing his friends immediate comfort so that he could lead them to a greater dependence on him and reveal his glory to them by doing what only he could do. Jesus said, "Did I not tell you that if you believed you would see the glory of God?" (v 40). And they did.

I still long for relief and healing for my son and my family, and I did really need a job to provide for them, but the waiting increased my longing for more of Christ and his glory through our lives, even at the cost of earthly comfort. That would never have happened if Jesus had healed my son as a toddler or answered when I first prayed for a job. He has loved me enough to delay. And he has loved me enough to allow the death of so much in me (my strength, comfort, desire for success, and self-confidence) in order to bring me greater life in him and bring glory to himself.

I've had many conversations with those who are convinced that if we just claim the power of Jesus, our family will be healed, our wealth restored, and our suffering removed. If we name it and claim it, we'll have it. But there is no greater evidence of this being untrue than the life of Jesus himself. As the late theologian R.C. Sproul pointed out:

"Who will charge Jesus with failure to pray in faith? He prayed 'Take this cup from me. Nevertheless, not my will, but yours, be done.' God said no. The way of suffering was the Father's plan."
(Surprised by Suffering, page 17)

Jesus prayed with more faith than any of us—and God said no. Sometimes, it's for our good and God's glory for us to wait. That doesn't make it easy to wait. But it makes it possible to do so.

2. CHRIST IS WORKING IN THE WAITING

Mary and Martha believed that Jesus had the power to heal, and they knew that he loved them. So how confusing it must have been when Jesus chose to delay in such a way that by the time he arrived, their brother had died.

Do you ever feel that way? Are you longing for healing or growth in your relationship with your spouse, but the longer you wait, the more impossible it seems? Have you prayed for answers and for assurance of God's presence, while feeling nothing but silence? Do you believe Jesus has the power to change your situation, and wonder why he has not done so? You're not alone; Mary wondered this very thing:

Now when Mary came to where Jesus was and saw him, she fell at his feet, saying to him, "Lord, if you had been here, my brother would not have died." When Jesus saw her weeping, and the Jews who had come with her also weeping, he was deeply moved in his spirit and greatly troubled. And he said, "Where have you laid him?" They said to him, "Lord, come and see." Jesus wept. (John 11 v 32-35)

Here's what we must not miss: though Jesus let Lazarus die, he also came alongside the sisters, grieved with them, wept with them, and spoke with them. Despite his foreknowledge of what was best for their eternal good, he still felt and mourned the pain that Lazarus' death brought.

Friend, Jesus does not leave you to wait alone. He grieves with you in the waiting, even as he is sovereign over the waiting. "What is my strength, that I should wait?" asked Job (6 v 11). "Our Lord and Savior, Jesus Christ," we can answer.

3. WAITING IS ACTIVE

God doesn't call us to sit idly by as we wait on his leading or answer. Nor is he idle—he accomplishes his purposes in and around us through the waiting. Here are three things we can actively do while we have to wait.

1. *Pursue God in his word.* As we wait and seek his presence, he will satisfy our longings, and we will come to find more joy in him than in the answers we seek.

2. *Pursue God in prayer.* Our cries for help, our pleading for answers, and our desperate longing for wisdom and strength will not fall on deaf ears with our Savior. We are to pray humbly, but we can also pray confidently. Perhaps a time of waiting is the best season in which to learn truly to do this: "Let us then with confidence draw near to the throne of grace, that we may receive mercy and find grace to help in the time of need" (Hebrews 4 v 16).

3. *Take the next step.* Elisabeth Elliot, the wife of the missionary martyr Jim Elliot, liked to quote a poem:

   "Many a questioning, many a fear,
   Many a doubt, hath its quieting here.
   Moment by moment, let down from heaven,
   Time, opportunity, and guidance are given.

Fear not tomorrows, child of the King,
Trust them with Jesus, do the next thing."

Instead of focusing on the end result, be willing to walk by faith, one step at a time. Instead of wondering what route the path will take, take the next step and trust that he has laid out the direction. "Consider the work of God: who can make straight what he has made crooked?" (Ecclesiastes 7 v 13). It's better to follow our Savior on the crooked path than find a straight path and have no Savior.

In a very real sense, all of the Christian life is waiting— waiting for glory. Since we know it's coming, and we know it's in God's timing, we can wait eagerly and patiently (Romans 8 v 23-25). Our painful seasons of waiting in this life can, if nothing else, teach us to wait well in our age of instant gratification—to walk by faith and cling to Christ throughout this life as we wait for glory.

"What is the end, that I should be patient?" asked Job (6 v 11). "The promise of the glory of God and the joy of being in his presence for all eternity," we can answer.

And until then, we wait.

REFLECT

- What are you currently waiting for? Is there anything that the Lord has shown you through the story of Lazarus or Job that gives you hope and encouragement in your current season of waiting?
- If you feel stuck where you are and don't understand why you have seen no leading or answer from the Lord, what is one step you can practically take today in order to do the next thing?

- (Together, if possible) Share with your spouse one practical area, and one area of your relationship with God, where you have struggled the most in your season of waiting. Share with one another what you have learned from this time—and/or from this chapter—that you want to use to help you wait well going forward.

PRAY

Heavenly Father, waiting is hard and discouraging, and can feel pointless. At times, I wonder if you hear my desperate pleas for help and, if you do, why you seem to remain silent. I am weak and unable to go on in my limited strength and understanding. If you won't remove the struggle from me, I need your strength to endure and the faith to trust you through this. As I look at the life of Jesus, I'm reminded that even he waited and suffered—and that in your timing and way, you brought about your perfect will through his life. Please let that give me confidence and hope that you are doing the same in my life. Today, help me trust and rest in the truth that you hear my voice and will give me the strength that I need, and that you see my pain and are grieving with me. Help me to believe that you won't delay one minute longer than what is necessary for my good and for your glory to be shown through it. Use my waiting to draw my heart to a greater dependence on you and a deeper longing for the day when I will be in your presence for all eternity. Amen.

For further meditation: Psalm 61 v 1-2; Psalm 147 v 10-11; Lamentations 3 v 18-26; Habakkuk 2 v 2-4; Ephesians 5 v 5-6.

Journaling

_____

_____

_____

_____

_____

_____

_____

_____

_____

_____

_____

_____

_____

_____

_____

_____

_____

_____

_____

_____

_____

_____

CHAPTER 11

The Strange Gift of Lamenting

*Remember that my life is a breath; my eye will
never again see good ... Therefore I will not
restrain my mouth; I will speak in the anguish
of my spirit; I will complain in the bitterness
of my soul. (Job 7 v 7, 11)*

Lament. It brings two worlds together—an honest wrestling with pain and confusion, and a growing trust and renewed hope in the promises of God. Through our laments we can shepherd our hearts and our words to move from questioning and complaining to hope-filled worship. Lament moves us to a real and realistic trust in God's character and promises despite our unchanged circumstances.

Unfortunately, lament is a somewhat lost art for Christians. It's something that I have only recently started to understand the nature and value of.

Lamenting doesn't come naturally to Western Christians, surrounded as we are in our culture with messages such as "Be strong and independent," "Suffering is a sign of weakness," and "Think positive." Our society (and often our church) is uncomfortable with suffering, too often giving pat answers for our pain and expecting us to quickly move on from it. For men, lament is even harder, because we're

Culturally we have very little framework for what to do when life hurts, and in church we often skip to songs of praise but rarely sing songs of lament.

taught to find our identity in being strong and capable leaders of our home. Admitting that our world is not ok means admitting our weaknesses and lack of control. That's hard, and it's counter-cultural.

So culturally we have very little framework for what to do when life hurts. In church, we often skip to songs of worship and praise (which are right and good), yet we rarely sing songs of lament, by which we worship through the acknowledgment of grief and pain. But if we cannot lament, then, as the Christian musician and author Michael Card suggests, we will miss out on "the forsaken sense of suffering [that pain] causes and find a substitute for intimacy with God," and we will not learn to "stubbornly refuse to let go of the loneliness and continue on the path toward an ever-increasing, continuously painful [yet] unheard-of intimacy with God" (*A Sacred Sorrow*, page 65).

Thankfully, the book of Job shows us what godly lament looks like. It shows us that God longs for us to come to him in our brokenness, pouring out our pain and confusion to him who is able to bear our burdens upon himself. Lament is the vehicle that allows our fumbling words and raw pain to be brought before our God in honesty and dependence on the Holy Spirit, and to lay claim to the truth and promises of God's word.

Lamenting is not merely complaining about the pain in our life, as non-believers might (and all of us do at times); it's an open invitation to bring our honest cries of suffering to our Father. Christian lament is different because, even as we pour out our grief, we can know that grief no longer has the last word. Non-believers can grieve, but without Christ their grief is no more than the acknowledgment of their pain. Worldly lament cannot look beyond itself because it has no hope. But God's word says that there is a better way: that we do not grieve as those with no hope

(1 Thessalonians 4 v 13). Choosing to rehearse what we know to be true about God and proclaiming his character back to him through our laments gives us an exit ramp from the cycle of complaining and confusion, and puts us on the path that will lead to deeper trust and greater hope as we take our eyes off of our circumstances and direct them heavenward. As pastor Mark Vroegop describes, lament is "a prayer in pain that leads to trust ... the language for living between the poles of a hard life and trusting in God's sovereignty. Without lament we won't know how to process pain" (*Dark Clouds, Deep Mercy*, page 21).

So how do we put lament into practice? I'd like to draw out for you what this looks like, so that you can grow to see the gift that biblical lament is to us.

Throughout Job (along with Lamentations and the psalms of lament), we see three stages of prayer that we can model in our own lives.

1. TAKE YOUR THOUGHTS DIRECTLY TO GOD

When Job's initial suffering and loss hits, he brings his anguish and confusion to his friends by wrestling with the purpose of his suffering. He laments, "Why did I not die at birth, come out from the womb and expire?" (Job 3 v 11). Job continues by voicing his torment as he changes the direction of his words from his friends toward God:

> *Therefore I will not restrain my mouth; I will speak in the anguish of my spirit; I will complain in the bitterness of my soul ... I loathe my life; I would not live forever. Leave me alone, for my days are a breath ... How long will you not look away from me nor leave me alone till I swallow my spit?*
>
> *(Job 7 v 11, 16, 19)*

In all of Job's complaining, he is not rejected by God; his spiritual outpouring and questioning is heard by God, who responds to it at the appropriate time. There came a point when Job stopped talking about God and started talking to him. His lamenting was not a sign of weak faith or a rebellious heart toward God, but rather of a heart that confidently trusted in the merciful ear of his heavenly Father.

Though we must be careful that we don't come to God simply to shake our angry fists at him, tell him he's got it wrong, and walk away in distrust, we do have the freedom and privilege to bring our grief and questions directly to our heavenly Father. We can ask, "Why?" and we can ask, "How long?" and we can ask, "Where are you, Father?"

Brother or sister, what do you need to bring to God in honesty today? If you aren't sure how to find the words to say, begin by praying the Psalms and you will be given language for your lament. Here are few to get you started: Psalms 4, 10, 13, 22, 39, 42 – 43, and 102. Start by praying these back to God; and, if your spouse is willing, spend some time praying through them together. It's often a struggle to put words to our struggles, but as Christians we have the Spirit of God, who "helps us in our weakness. For we do not know what to pray for as we ought, but the Spirit himself intercedes for us with groanings too deep for words" (Romans 8 v 26).

2. CALL TRUTH TO MIND

Bridge the gap from pain to trust. As in the book of Job, in the third chapter of Lamentations we find a believer who is greatly afflicted. He cries out in honest lament:

> *[God] has walled me about so that I cannot escape;*
> *he has made my chains heavy;*
> *though I call and cry for help,*

> *he shuts out my prayer;*
> *he has blocked my ways with blocks of stones;*
> *he has made my paths crooked.*
>
> (Lamentations 3 v 7-9)

He grasps for words that sufficiently describe his anguish and confusion over what God's sovereignty has allowed. But, as with all godly laments, we then see him turn from his pain and fight for hope in what he knows to be true: "My soul continually remembers it and is bowed down within me. *But this I call to mind*, and therefore I have hope" (v 20-21, my emphasis). *Calling to mind* is a conscious choice. It's a fight to lift our eyes from the ash heap and look beyond it to the glory of God's throne. It's choosing to think about and trust in God's steadfast love, goodness, and faithfulness. It's choosing to believe that because "he does not willingly bring affliction or grief" (v 33, NIV), there is hope in and beyond our pain, even if we can't make sense of the path that is taking us there. When all we can see is the darkness of night, we can still trust that "the steadfast love of the LORD never ceases; his mercies never come to an end; they are new every morning; great is your faithfulness" (v 22-23).

We must speak the promises and character of God to ourselves and wait upon the Lord, believing that there will be a day when he will judge, he will redeem, and he will make all things right. We grieve because our pain is real, but we have hope because Jesus is greater than our pain and sorrow.

3. RECEIVE THE STRENGTH AND JOY OF THE LORD

As we stand in the gap between our pain and the hope and comfort we find in Christ, the soil of our suffering can begin to sprout forth seeds of joy, renewed strength, and a peace that's beyond our own understanding. Of course, this isn't a one-time magic bullet. But as time goes on, the process of lament will often bring us more quickly from complaint and grief to finding joy and rest in God's promises once again. This strength is not found in our circumstances changing or in pretending our difficulties don't exist, but rather in the Lord's promise that he is with us and will redeem and restore all things. This joy launches us out of complaining and questioning and brings us to the blessing that can only be found in knowing and resting in Jesus Christ. We lay our griefs on him, and he bestows his strength and joy on us.

TALK TO GOD, NOT JUST ABOUT GOD

Throughout all of Job, we never see his friends address God directly in prayer. Instead, they attempt to talk on God's behalf. They think they have all the answers, so they never stop to ask for help. Their perceived wisdom was actually their foolishness because it was based on their own understanding rather than humble dependence on God to comfort their friend. Had they chosen to lament alongside of Job and pray on his behalf, they would have had the privilege of drawing nearer to the Lord and truly comforting their friend in his misery.

Of course, it isn't wrong to share our struggles and our thoughts with our spouse and those around us; but we will only experience the power and blessing of lament when we bring our sorrows to Christ, the only one who has shoulders broad enough to bear our burdens, and the power and wisdom to heal our hearts and give us hope.

Job's friends talked to Job about God; Job talked to God about Job. And we must talk to God about ourselves. You can encourage your spouse to do so, too, by praying with them. Though this may be hard to start with, or may be met with resistance, it's worth continuing to offer this and continuing to grow in. If you feel too paralyzed to pray, or you struggle to find the words, try simply writing a prayer down, or use Scripture to give you words to pray. Don't grow frustrated when you can't capture your feelings verbally—the Spirit will do what you cannot. And when your husband or wife can't find words, pray over them. Set a prayer time each day to pray together—even if five minutes is all you can manage, it will make a huge difference.

REAL HOPE LIES HERE

Christian, the worst thing we can do is give God the silent treatment. Come to him honestly, trusting that he already knows the state of your heart. Share with him the confusion, pain, and questions swirling in your soul. Rehearse his promises to you in Scripture and remind yourself of his goodness, faithfulness, and love. Then ask him to help you walk forward in faith, trusting who he is rather than what you can make sense of. This is lament—real about what you face today, but with hope for your eternal future. By God's grace and with the help of the Holy Spirit, may he enable us to glorify him by praising him in the darkness and trusting him in the silence.

REFLECT

- Have you gone through a time in your life when you felt as though prayer "didn't work," so you gave up praying? What have you wrongly believed about God and his promises that is now keeping you silent, resigned to your circumstances, and unwilling to persevere in prayer?
- Does the idea of lament make you uncomfortable? If so, why is that? In what ways might biblical lamenting help you to cling to Christ through your struggles?

- (Together, if possible) What keeps you from praying together (if you don't)? What are some practical steps you can take to implement prayer (and lament) in your life as a couple? Share with your spouse any insecurities you feel in this area and spend some time praying together, asking God to grow this area of your marriage. (If your spouse is unwilling, spend some time thanking Jesus that he sees you and will provide all you need, and pray that he would draw your spouse's heart to himself.)

PRAY

He has walled me about so that I cannot escape;
  he has made my chains heavy;
though I call and cry for help,
  he shuts out my prayer ...
My soul is bereft of peace;
  I have forgotten what happiness is;
so I say, "My endurance has perished;
  so has my hope from the LORD."
Remember my affliction and my wanderings ...
My soul continually remembers it
  and is bowed down within me.
But this I call to mind,
  and therefore I have hope:
The steadfast love of the LORD never ceases;
  his mercies never come to an end;
they are new every morning;
  great is your faithfulness.
"The LORD is my portion," says my soul,
  "therefore I will hope in him."
The LORD is good to those who wait for him,
  to the soul who seeks him.

It is good that one should wait quietly
*for the salvation of the L*ORD*. Amen.*
(From Lamentations 3 v 7-8, 17-19a, 20-26)

For further meditation: Psalms 10, 28, 55; Lamentations 3;
Mark 14 v 32-42; Colossians 4 v 2.

Journaling

_____

_____

_____

_____

_____

_____

_____

_____

_____

_____

_____

_____

_____

_____

_____

_____

_____

_____

_____

_____

_____

_____

CHAPTER 12

Walking the Valley of Despair Hand in Hand

I loathe my life; I would not live forever. Leave me alone, for my days are but a breath … My spirit is broken; my days are extinct; the graveyard is ready for me. (Job 7 v 16; 17 v 1)

"I can't live like this anymore! I just want to die!" I cried out through sobs. I sat on our bed across from Jeff's work desk and tried to make sense of what was going on inside of me. I guess he was trying to make sense of it too.

I was tired of the chronic pain, the frequent bouts of illness, and the weariness of dealing with the kids' struggles, but what broke me was the torture of being a prisoner of my own mind—trapped in a perpetual sense of darkness. Part of me wished my breath would just stop coming.

As I struggled to express to Jeff the painful reality of living with a constant cloud of depression, I read to him Zack Eswine's words from *Spurgeon's Sorrows* as an attempt to explain my own internal battle.

"Painful circumstances or a disposition of gloom within our chemistry can put on their muddy boots and stand thick, full weighted and heavy upon our tired chests. It is almost like anxiety is tying a rope around our ankles and hands of our breath. Tied to a

*chair, with the lights out, we sit swallowing in panic
the dark air.*

*"These kinds of circumstances and bodily chemistry
steal the gifts of divine love too, as if all of God's love
letters and picture albums are burning up in a fire just
outside the door, a fire which we are helpless to stop.
We sit there, helpless in the dark of divine absence, tied
to this chair, present only to ash and wheeze, while
all we hold dear seems lost forever. We even wonder if
we've brought this all on ourselves. It's our fault. God is
against us. We've forfeited God's help." (page 18)*

The valley of despair is a very real place, and it's one that
strong Christians are not exempt from. For some, illness
creates a brokenness within their mind, bringing on a clin-
ical depression that is just as real as an illness that sickens
the body. For others, intense grief, overwhelming circumstances, resisting God's heavy hand drawing them toward
repentance, and various other triggers can lead to a season of
despair (for more in-depth help in understanding the differences, I highly recommend David Murray's book, *Christians
Get Depressed Too*). It can be difficult to distinguish between
the two, and to some extent they need to be approached
differently—but what they have in common is that they are
both a place of deep emotional and spiritual wrestling.

Sometimes despair is linked to circumstances. Sometimes,
it isn't. As C.H. Spurgeon described it:

*"Quite involuntarily, unhappiness of mind, depression
of spirit, and sorrow of heart will come upon you. You
may be without any real reason for grief, and yet may
become among the most unhappy of men because, for
the time, your body has conquered your soul."*
(The Saddest Cry from the Cross, page 656)

If you or your spouse have experienced this, you are in good company. Job, after initially responding with an unshakable faith in the immediate aftermath of his loss, suddenly found himself walking in the valley of despair as his suffering continued, desiring the grave and unsure of who God was anymore.

> *When I say, "My bed will comfort me, my couch will ease my complaint," then you scare me with dreams and terrify me with visions, so that I would choose strangling and death rather than my bones. I loathe my life; I would not live forever. Leave me alone, for my days are but a breath … My spirit is broken; my days are extinct; the graveyard is ready for me.*
> *(Job 7 v 13-16; 17 v 1)*

Thank God that he gives us a glimpse into the darkest days of Job's life. It assures us that we aren't alone in our battle with despair, and it helps us keep perspective when we struggle to feel God's presence on our darkest days. Whether we are battling depression or are trying to encourage our spouse who is, we need to fight to hold onto these truths...

OUR FEELINGS DON'T DEFINE THE TRUTH

When you feel despair in your physical or mental being (often with a distorted view of reality), it's easy to believe that it's a sign of God's displeasure with you. Though at times we may feel the heavy hand of God upon us in order to draw us into repentance (Psalm 32), depression often fills our mind with lies, tempting us to believe that our feelings are an accurate picture of our relationship with Christ and others. If we feel unlovable, we must be unloved. If we feel hopelessness, we must be hopeless. If we feel lonely, we must have been abandoned. And if we feel shame, we must be unforgiven.

But, as readers of the book of Job, we know that Job's view that God was against him was not how things really were. How he felt was not what was true. And the Lord kept him from losing all hope as he walked through the valley of despair: "Though he slay me, I will yet hope in him" (Job 13 v 15). God had not, in fact, "slain" him—the work was Satan's (2 v 7); but what is crucial is that Job did not finish his sentence there. He somehow still believed that the Lord was to be trusted and that there was therefore hope for him.

I will hope in him. Brother or sister, however we feel about God, we too have to constantly keep the truth of salvation in front of us to fight back against all that bombards us from within. No matter how we may feel or how things may appear, if we are new creations in Christ Jesus we are loved, accepted, and forgiven. A few Scriptures that have been particularly helpful to keep in front of me are Psalm 3 v 3; Psalm 23 v 1-6; Psalm 40 v 1-3; Isaiah 61 v 3; John 16 v 33; 2 Corinthians 12 v 9; Revelation 21 v 4.

DEPRESSION IS NOT A SIGN THAT GOD IS ABSENT

Depression can cause us to feel an unimaginable sense of loneliness. Not only do we feel as if the world is going on without us, but we can even feel strange to ourselves, as if we lost who we once were. And God seems distant, too: "Behold, I go forward, but he is not there, and backward, but I do not perceive him" (Job 23 v 8).

Depression and despair tell us that our suffering and feelings are proof of God's absence, and yet, as we see in Job, God isn't far off. Little did Job know that his suffering, which seemed to be due to God's wrath, actually came about as a result of the Lord boasting in Job's godliness, as a proud father boasts of his child. And soon, the God of the universe would speak directly to his child. God was not absent.

When our feelings argue God's absence, we need to argue back with the truth:

> *O LORD, you have searched me and known me!*
> *You know when I sit down and when I rise up;*
> * you discern my thoughts from afar.*
> *You search out my path and my lying down*
> * and are acquainted with all my ways.*
> *Even before a word is on my tongue,*
> * behold, O LORD, you know it altogether.*
> (Psalm 139 v 1-4)

Jesus did not come down from heaven, suffer, and die for a world that rejected him, defeating death for any who would believe, only to abandon us when life gets hard. No, he sacrificed himself to reconcile us to himself and to open a way for us to have relationship with a holy God. This is the confidence of our hope when our feelings tell us otherwise.

As Zack Eswine writes:

> *"Though our bodily gloom allows us no feeling of His tender touch, He holds on to us still. Our feelings of Him do not save us. He does. Our hope, therefore, does not reside in our ability to preserve a good mood but in His ability to bear us up. Jesus will never abandon us with our downcast heart."*
> (Spurgeon's Sorrows, page 38-39)

DEPRESSION DOESN'T MAKE US USELESS

When despondency strips from us our natural ability to see and feel hope, joy, and purpose in our sorrow, we have a tendency to view everything as a confirmation of our uselessness. If our kids act out, it seems to confirm that we've failed as a parent. If our spouse or friend gently points out an area of weakness or sin in our life, we think, "See, I can't do *anything* right!" Sometimes, all it takes is one mistake or setback for us to conclude that everything is against us and it's useless even to try anymore. We have nothing to give. Here is where it's crucial that we look to God's word for our value, rather than to the world or our own standards. One passage that I meditate on often when I'm battling with feelings of uselessness is Psalm 147 v 10-11:

> *His delight is not in the strength of the horse,*
> *nor his pleasure in the legs of a man,*
> *but the* LORD *favors those who fear him,*
> *in those who hope for his steadfast love.*

There is no Christian whom God does not love, is not pleased with, and cannot use. In fact, a season (or a lifetime) of feeling a keen sense of our inadequacies can be an opportunity to look to Jesus to give us our sense of worth and our confidence in serving him. Job longed for the grave, but thousands of years after he faced his valley of despair, he is still providing hope to millions—including you and me. God was doing far more than Job could see or feel. He is still doing so today, in your life.

THROUGH THE VALLEY TOGETHER

If you are the one who is trying to navigate loving your husband or wife who is battling depression, I'm so grateful for you. Please know you are not left to your own resources. Christ has chosen you as your spouse's partner to walk through this valley alongside them—not to fix them, but to love, fight for and serve them, and point them to Christ. It's not an easy calling, and it requires the grace and strength of the Lord to enable you to have the wisdom, grace, patience, and love that you need for this challenging journey.

First, remember that your spouse simply can't see what you do, or think as clearly as you can. I have tried to share my internal struggle with Jeff in this way:

> *"You and I might be sitting in the same room, and you might be sitting comfortably in a t-shirt, while I'm sitting next to you in three layers and still feeling cold. Your body is able to regulate body temperate as it should, while my health challenges mean that my body constantly struggles to regulate its temperature accurately. You can try to convince me that the room is warm all you want, even showing me the thermostat, but that doesn't change the reality that I feel cold."*

Personally, in seasons when I am battling depression, I find it isn't helpful for Jeff to try to convince me that reality is different than what I see and feel. Now, that doesn't mean he should just commiserate with me and my despairing thoughts, and it doesn't mean that he shouldn't gently point me to the truth at the appropriate time. But it is always more helpful for him to first listen and respond with compassion and empathy, asking questions and helping me bring the darkness of my thoughts into the light. When he knows that his job isn't to change me and that he won't be able to fully understand, he can support me by being a safe place for me to process my confusion and pain, helping me carry the burden as though it is our burden to carry together, rather than viewing it as a problem he just needs to fix (Galatians 6 v 2). But the only way he is able to help carry my burden is if he's consistently in God's word and looking to Christ for his own strength, wisdom, and comfort. He can pray for me (on his own and with me) and encourage me to bring my hurting heart to Christ and keep reading his word.

Second, hope for the best but be prepared for a long walk. One of the challenges of loving a spouse through depression or despair is the temptation to put a time limit on it. We may be patient for a time, but when our self-allotted time has passed (winter months are through... the circumstances have eased up... it's been over a year... the kids are older now...) and the battle continues, our patience can begin to wane. You need to sign up for the long haul. Your spouse needs to know you'll be there—so you need to pray to God for an end to the season, but also for his love to flow into and through you throughout this season.

Lastly, remember that it is not a defeat to seek help—be that from a pastor or a counselor (or, at times, a doctor). It's a sign that you want to love your spouse by walking through whatever the Lord allows as lovingly as you can. It need not define your marriage, and you can worship God in the way you walk alongside your spouse in this season that likely neither of you imagined when you said your vows.

I WILL YET HOPE

Suffering brother and sister, lift your heavy hearts. As C.H. Spurgeon, who knew all too well the weight of living with long-term depression and chronic pain, once said:

> *"We need patience under pain and hope under depression of spirit ... Our God ... will either make the burden lighter or the back stronger; he will diminish the need or increase the supply."*
> *(Sword and Trowel, page 15)*

I will yet hope in him.

REFLECT

- If you battle depression of one kind or another, do you struggle to believe one or more of the statements that are the subheadings in this chapter? What do you need to pray about? Write down the promises that you need to remind yourself of daily. What practical steps can you take to pursue the help and support you may need (emotionally, spiritually, medically, and so on)?
- If your spouse struggles with depression, when is it hardest for you? How can you get the support you need? In what specific way can you love your spouse today?
- (Together, if possible) Discuss your questions, struggles, and confusion revolving around the struggle with depression, and any practical steps you can take together to seek the help and support you may need in the areas mentioned in the first question.

PRAY

If you battle depression or feel despairing:

Lord, sometimes this darkness feels like too much to bear. I know what is true, but the inner noise and turmoil are frequently drowning that out. I believe you love me, yet I struggle to feel it. I believe you are good, but I struggle to see your goodness through the fog. I believe you can free me from this anguish, yet you have chosen not to. Jesus, if it is your will, lift these dark clouds and help me see the light of your goodness and love shining upon me. But if you don't, help me believe it when I can't feel it. Help me trust your promises when the brokenness of my mind and body tell me otherwise, and give me the strength to love and care for my husband/wife with a love that's beyond my own. Amen.

If your spouse battles depression or feels despairing:

Lord Jesus, I want to love my spouse well, but at times I struggle to know how. My encouragement and words seem unable to penetrate his/her darkened view of life, and it's easy for me to become impatient when I struggle to understand and relate to his/her inward suffering. Help me listen well and bear his/her burden in the way you have called me to. Forgive me when I respond out of my pride and selfishness, and please use this struggle to grow me in your likeness. Give me your compassion and patience, and help me honor you in how I care for, serve, and love him/her through this. Amen.

For further meditation: Psalm 30 v 1-5; Psalm 40 v 1-3; Psalm 42 v 11; Isaiah 41 v 10; Romans 8 v 38-39.

Journaling

CHAPTER 13

When Your Pasts Threaten Your Present

*For you write bitter things against me and make
me inherit the iniquities of my youth.
(Job 13 v 26)*

Last week, Sarah and I were in the kitchen when I noticed a pile of papers lying on the counter. My eyes landed on a sentence from one of Sarah's old journal entries. My heart felt heavy as I read her reflection of some shocking and descriptive words that were made to her by a group of guys during some dark days in her past. I tossed the papers down in disgust and asked her why she even kept these. Seeing my irritation rising, she said, her tone matching my anger, "That's the problem with you—you can't even talk about these things."

I thought, "Why am I the problem? What did I do?" This wasn't our first heated conversation about her past and my response to it. It was like being stuck in an endless cycle.

After taking some time to cool off, I asked Sarah to clarify what she meant by her response. As we discussed it in a (fairly) calm way, it dawned on me that my anger toward the sin of those guys was coming across to Sarah as though it was directed at her, leading her to feel renewed guilt and shame. Through my spoken and unspoken words, she felt as Job did about his friends: as though I was "writing bitter things against" her and making her "inherit the iniquities [and pain] of [her] youth." This was particularly hurtful to her because those "iniquities" had been visited upon her, not caused by her. In my struggle with her past, I was unintentionally weighing her down with her past shame, hurt, and guilt.

I felt—I feel—awful for what she has endured. But I had been majoring on how it was affecting our marriage and therefore impacting me, rather than seeing the full effect it had on her. Without ever meaning it to, my anger and frustration over her past was causing her to thicken her walls of self-protection.

I knew I was wrong.

By God's grace, that day he gave me a greater understanding of the shame and pain that Sarah had been carrying. What she wanted and needed to know (and hear) from me was that I saw her with eyes of love and grieved what she had suffered, rather than seeing her as the problem. She needed compassion and empathy, not judgment and anger, and certainly not more shame. She needed to know that I could love and accept all of her, including her painful past, just as Christ has. Her past is her story, and God's story, and is a vital part of her testimony of God's powerful work of redemption, not only in her life but in mine.

Praise God that he is a God of healing. Whatever baggage you or your spouse may have brought into marriage, and whoever's iniquity it was that created those burdens, there is always hope for redemption. For us, that has taken time and hasn't been easy. Here are three things that I've had to learn and still need actively to remember as we navigate this struggle within our marriage.

Whatever baggage you may have brought into marriage, there is always hope for redemption.

WE ARE ALL EQUAL BEFORE GOD

It isn't uncommon for one or both of us to enter into marriage with past sin and hurts—and that can easily lead to false beliefs and an unhealthy view of one another. For example, one spouse may view themselves as inferior (or more sinful) because of their past, causing them to live with a sense of shame, sometimes elevating their spouse to a place of unhealthy and idolatrous expectations.

On the flip side, deep down a spouse can be proud that their past is less sinful than their spouse's, leading to a lack of compassion and a sense of spiritual superiority. That sets the marriage up for bitterness, defeat, and a lack of intimacy and trust.

This also happens within a marriage when the sinful actions of one member of a couple tear at the marriage and deeply hurt the other. We'll speak more to that in chapter 24 on forgiveness, but the danger of viewing ourselves as inferior or superior, depending on whether we've done the wronging or been the one wronged, is worth recognizing.

The truth is, before we are able to love our spouse well—whether or not we are the one bringing the baggage (or the one who has caused the baggage)—we need to ask God for an accurate view of what our own heart would be like without Christ's saving work. For, as Paul memorably put it to Timothy:

> *The saying is trustworthy and deserving of full*
> *acceptance, that Christ Jesus came into the world to*
> *save sinners, of whom I am the foremost.*
>
> *(1 Timothy 1 v 15)*

We are all sinners. None of us is "better" than another sinner, and it is God's undeserved kindness where he has protected us from being harmed at the hand of another's sinful actions, or protected us from giving in to our own sinful desires. Fundamentally and universally, both spouses in a marriage are sinners. And wonderfully, anyone who trusts Jesus is a saved sinner. Brother, sister, it's not until our eyes are opened to how truly sinful we are that we can see ourselves as equally broken, yet in Christ as equally forgiven, as our spouse. If you are bringing the baggage, you need to realize that Paul's saying is true of you—yes, you're deeply sinful, but, yes, you're wonderfully saved. And if you are living with your spouse's baggage, it's only when you can accept that Paul's saying is true of you, too, that you will be able to see your husband or wife with greater compassion and extend the comfort they need as you walk with them through the pain they carry from their past.

There is a fine line between a healthy, righteous anger over past sin and its painful consequences in our marriage, and a self-righteous anger that makes us most bothered by its impact on us: self-righteous anger so blinds us that we use our spouse's sin to ignore or excuse our own ("Ok, but it's not like I've done what *you* did"; "Yes, but the biggest problem we have is that *you* can't move on"); and that results in a failure to respond with grace and compassion (Ephesians 4 v 26-27).

Guard against the temptation to think you deserve a better marriage or an easier life because of something you have done or not done. Whatever lies in the past, the truth for all God's people is that our sin, pain, and shame have been paid for and redeemed by the blood of Jesus on the cross.

JESUS WILL MAKE ALL THINGS RIGHT

If someone we love has been wronged by another person, it's natural to want to make the wrong right. The late theologian and counselor David Powlison helpfully describes our struggle:

"We are wired by God to operate in anger's logic: 'That matters, and it's wrong. It displeases me, and I am against it. I must change it, remove it, destroy it.' The core is that something important is not the way it's meant to be, and we are moved to action."
(Anger in Action, The Journal of Biblical Counseling, Fall 2006, Vol. 24, page 24)

However, while it is right to want justice, we must be careful not to put ourselves in the place of God, who alone has the knowledge and wisdom to judge justly. Paul guides us to "never avenge yourselves, but leave it to the wrath of God" (Romans 12 v 19). Instead of looking for ways to repay the evil that's been done, or dreaming of what we'd like to say or do to those who hurt our spouse if we only had the chance, we must remember that we serve a just God. He promises to deliver us from the pain of living in a fallen world, and that one day he will judge everyone according to what they have done here on this earth.

Job knew what it was like to feel (rightly) innocent, yet also ashamed: "Even if I am righteous, I cannot lift up my head. I am filled with shame and have drunk deeply of my affliction" (Job 10 v 15, CSB). Maybe you can relate to feeling beaten down and weak, ready to wave the white flag over your marriage because you can't fight the weight of the shame and the anger anymore. Rather than pushing down your shame, avoiding its presence, or being dominated by it, you can acknowledge it and then lay it at the feet of Jesus, knowing that what you have had done to you (or have yourself done) makes no difference to his view of you or love for you. And rather than holding onto your anger, you can trust God to bring justice, which means that you don't need to, for you know that one day, the One who died to make you right with him will make all things right in this world.

THE PAST NEED NOT HAVE THE LAST WORD

After fifteen years of wanting to help but only making things harder for Sarah, I praise God for enabling us to see ourselves more rightly, to talk to each other more gently, and to face the pain of Sarah's past together. If I could, I would say to those who sinned against her and heaped such unmerited shame on her, "As for you, you meant evil against [my wife], but God meant it for good" (Genesis 50 v 20). By God's grace, he is enabling me still to hate what was done, and to trust in God's greater purpose at work within the culprits. It wasn't until I gave up my desire to fix it and move past it— as well as see the selfishness in my irritation at the impact it was having on me and our marriage, and focus on what it was doing to Sarah—that I was able to listen well, be a part of the healing process in our marriage, and love Sarah as I am called to. As the theologian A.W. Tozer said:

> *"Quite literally a new channel must be cut through*
> *the desert of our minds to allow the sweet waters of*
> *truth that will heal our great sickness to flow in."*
> *(The Knowledge of the Holy, page 104-105)*

Most marriages need to deal with baggage in one way or another. It can be painful, but it does not need to be buried unspoken about, or to dominate, brought up in every moment of tension or strain. If a painful past has been a struggle in your marriage, remember that we're all sinful, that Jesus will make all things right in his timing, and that both your pasts are a part of the story God is writing in your life—a story that, as you trust Jesus, includes forgiveness and freedom from shame, and will one day end with glorious, complete restoration and a righting of wrongs. The more you believe this, the more you'll be in a posture to listen well, to love well, to pray well, and to truly help one another. Then the pain of the past will not have the last word, for God will.

REFLECT

- Are there any areas in your spouse's past that you believe are causing your current struggles in your marriage? If so, are you bringing unnecessary shame or guilt on your spouse for any baggage that was brought into your marriage or even something from earlier days in your relationship? Do you need to ask for forgiveness from your spouse for the way you have been treating them?

- Do you ever see your spouse's sins as greater than your own, and/or responsible for the issues that you have in your marriage? To what extent is that fair?

- Do you live under the shame of your past? If so, how does the gospel bring hope and healing to your past sin and the sins committed against you? How do the many biblical accounts of God bringing beauty out of ashes or using what seems evil or painful in order to refine his people and make them holy encourage you about your marriage today?

- (Together, if possible) Discuss how your past has impacted who you are today and your relationship with each other. If you have felt shame in your marriage, gently share what has made you feel that way. If you recognize ways that you have held your spouse's past against them, confess it to the Lord and your spouse, and pray that God will give you a heart of humility, grace, and love toward your husband/wife. Pray together, thanking God that salvation through Jesus Christ purifies us from all sin—past, present, and future—and that we can walk in the peace, freedom, and joy that his forgiveness brings.

PRAY

Lord, you promise that when we come to Christ, you remove our sins as far as the east is from the west—not only mine, but my spouse's too. Help me to live in light of this truth in our marriage today. Lord, give me your strength to love my spouse well and to search my own heart for any sin that is hindering our marital oneness. Uproot any pride in my thinking or in my actions. Bring forgiveness where there have been sins that have been repented of, and bring your truth to our hearts and minds if we need to repent of unnoticed sins. May we find renewed hope in our marriage today as we see that you are greater than any of our sins and any of our past pain. Thank you that in your kindness we are not defined by our past, and that we can find hope and healing and change in walking through life together with you. Amen.

For further meditation: Genesis 50 v 15-21; Isaiah 43 v 16-19; John 8 v 1-11; Romans 2 v 1-3; Philippians 3 v 12-14.

Journaling

CHAPTER 14

Who Am I Now? Identity Crisis and Your Marriage

He has walled up my way, so that I cannot pass,
and he has set darkness upon my paths. He has
stripped from me my glory and taken the crown
from my head. He breaks me down on every side,
and I am gone. (Job 19 v 8-10)

It's been six months since I've been able to fully walk on my own. A severe injury to my ankle nearly two decades ago has slowly been taking away my ability to walk, leaving me couch-ridden after my fifth surgery in hopes of restoring as much walking ability as possible. As a mom to four young children, losing my ability to walk makes me unsure of the future in a whole new way. Throughout these past several months, I've not only battled new fears, but I've felt acutely the loss of my independence, as I have needed to depend on others to do even the most basic things.

The practical challenges and my increased loss of independence, however, haven't been the only source of frustration. I've wrestled with why God has allowed yet another loss—the loss of being able to do so many activities that he created me to enjoy. There are times—when Jeff goes out for a run, or a friend tells me about the sports league they're playing in, or I see the disappointment in my kids' eyes when I can't do something active with them—that a fresh wave of grief washes over me. I battle envy and sadness, because I'm grieving the loss of who I once was. I grew up accustomed to receiving praise for my athleticism; and being able to exercise and play sports was a stress-reliever for me. I was an athlete. Now I can't walk.

Because life is ever-changing and unpredictable, we will all experience seasons when we lose something we had based our identity on. Maybe you're a woman who used to find fulfillment and praise in your job, but now you find yourself endlessly working at home with unappreciative children and seemingly little to show for it. Maybe you're a guy who's feeling crippled because of joblessness or an unfulfilling position at work. Maybe you've longed to be a parent, but infertility, child loss, or special needs have left you feeling as though a part of you has died. Maybe you're struggling in your marriage itself because you'd dreamed of how marriage would be and, well, it's fallen quite short of that standard.

The problem is that when we find our sense of self and security in something that can change, we risk losing our sense of self if we lose it. If I think I'll be enough, or successful, or happy if I get something (health, kids, career, and so on) then if it doesn't come or it isn't all I've dreamed it would be, I won't just be disappointed; I'll be lost.

If it's marriage itself that most makes me feel valued and fulfilled, and our relationship begins to suffer, I'm either going to blame myself or my spouse (or both). If my marriage has to be perfect to make me feel good about myself, then any imperfection has the potential to cause conflict and even drive a wedge between me and my spouse. I'll become angry, frustrated, and tempted to look elsewhere for fulfillment.

Equally, if our sense of self is in something outside our marriage, then we may neglect our marriage to pursue whatever makes us feel good about ourselves (especially when marriage gets tough)—witness the husband or wife who chases a career promotion at the expense of their family, or seeks praise and connection online because they feel unfulfilled or unappreciated at home. If we lose the thing we are finding fulfillment and purpose in, it will tempt us to become sad, angry, and apathetic in a way that is bound to affect our marriage. I've seen this in myself at times. As I've lost the physical ability to do many of the things I found enjoyment and confidence in, I've struggled with managing my stress at home and not taking my frustrations out on Jeff. Similarly, during seasons when Jeff has struggled at work, at times I've felt as though he were unhappy and frustrated with me. Whether we are aware of it or not, placing our identity in marriage (or our spouse) will create unhealthy expectations, and a search for our identity in things outside of our marriage will often be hurtful to our spouse and damaging to our marriage.

HOW TO SPOT THE DEAD ENDS

It might be worth asking yourself a few questions:

- What do I think about to make me feel better on a bad day? How do I instinctively complete these sentences: "At least I've got…" or "It's ok because…"?
- If I had to describe myself in terms of four or five "I am" sentences, what would I say? If I were to lose one of those things, how would I feel?
- Am I placing my identity in my spouse and my marriage? Do I place unhealthy and unrealistic expectations on my spouse to meet my needs and satisfy me? Or does a job, hobby, talent, social media, or even ministry opportunities consume my time, thoughts, and energy to the point that my spouse only gets the leftovers? What

impact does my view of my marriage and those other things have on our relationship?

These are hard questions to ask, and they can be even harder to answer honestly. But we need to be honest, even if it's a bit humbling—because there is a better way, but we'll only be able to follow it if we've identified the dead-end roads we tend to walk down.

REDEEMED, SECURE, AND HEADING HOME

Job knew the loss of earthly identities. As a once well-respected, strong, and wealthy man, he now found himself ill, poor, and the laughing stock and object of judgment of those around him, including his wife and closest friends (Job 19 v 17-19). Job says of God:

> *He has stripped from me my glory and taken the crown from my head. He breaks me down on every side, and I am gone, and my hope has he pulled up like a tree. (v 9-10)*

Not only had his "glory"—the things that made him him—been stripped from Job, to the point where who he once was no longer existed, but Job also knew his suffering was in some sense God's doing. Trying to reconcile God's goodness with what he was experiencing was the essence of Job's struggle.

But here's what amazes me. Despite not understanding why God has stripped him of his earthly "glory," and while still grieving all that he has lost, Job suddenly declares with confidence (such confidence that he wanted his words inscribed in a book for all to see, v 23!):

> *I know that my Redeemer lives, and at the last he will stand upon the earth. And after my skin has been thus destroyed, yet in my flesh I shall see God,*

whom I shall see for myself, and my eyes shall behold, and not another. (v 25-27)

Somehow, in some way, the loss of his earthly "glory" had only served to increase Job's confidence in the God in whom he'd always trusted. What was happening? It's this: his identity could now no longer be found in anything of his own doing (including his marriage), but only in the promise that he would one day see the living God, who would redeem him and all that he had lost. If his purpose in life had been based on being wealthy, healthy, and loved by those around him, he would have had no reason to go on. But Job knew that his best life was yet to come. Job staked his confidence entirely in the hope and truth of God's unchanging character and promises, rather than his confusing, awful circumstances. He'd been stripped of his "glory," yet he had not lost what he most needed—and that was his true glory.

This is the hope we can have as well when we're faced with losses that appear to erase who we used to be and steal what we used to find our confidence from. There are three simple truths that all who are in Christ can, like Job, anchor themselves to:

1. *I'm redeemed.* I'm twice owned by God: first in creation, second in salvation. My life is not my own; I have been rescued from the curse and power of sin and empowered by the Holy Spirit to live in freedom to serve, love, worship, enjoy, reflect, and glorify Christ in all I do (19 v 23-25).

2. *I'm secure.* My Redeemer will return and, because I am declared righteous by the blood of Christ, I will live with him for eternity in complete wholeness. Even now, he is making me more like the person he designed me to be, as he changes me into his Son's likeness (19 v 26-27; 23 v 10).

3. *I'm heading home to Christ.* I will see him one day, and my faith will be turned to sight. Though I cannot always see and understand his ways, he is worthy to be trusted and will prove himself faithful. Today, I can live in view of that future day (23 v 13-15).

If we hold these three things at the core of our identity, we can cope with disappointments within marriage or losing things around our marriage with unassailable joy instead of anger, defeat, bitterness, or despair.

After all, in Christ we cannot lose what we truly need. And when loss brings anger, envy, and bitterness, it's because we're being detached from an idol. In hard times, it's sometimes easy to cling to an idol even as we lose an idol. I have found this to be an acute struggle in seasons of suffering because disappointment and heartache in one area of life can tempt me to cling to something else that makes me feel good, worthwhile, or confident. In storms, when one idol is taken from us, we can simply grasp another. But idols are cruel masters. They never satisfy or free us as they promise to. So in God's kindness, sometimes he challenges these idols and false identities, allowing us to feel the sting and emptiness of their false promises in order that we might put them back in their proper place. These storms can move us to find ourselves in Christ more, and therefore to not lose ourselves in the loss of something precious.

NO MORE PITY PARTIES

As painful as the loss of using my ankle has been, and as much as I'm tempted to throw a pity party from time to time, I can see how much God has used the loss of something good to give me something greater. Though athletics, being active, and running with my kids were gifts I once enjoyed, they never truly satisfied me, and they certainly didn't define me. But it took losing them, and grieving them, and allowing the pain of that to drive me closer to Christ, to realize that he has all that I need and can satisfy me in ways those things never could. In his kindness, as I've gradually accepted what I've lost and grown to understand that my identity and security are and could only ever be in Jesus, he's opened my eyes to new gifts and enjoyments, such as writing—an activity that I can do from the couch! But more than anything, I've learned that my security can't be in anything I do or anything I have, including in Jeff or in being Mrs Walton—it must always be in Christ and all that he has promised me. I've learned the truth of these words of Joni Eareckson Tada, who lost the use of all her limbs as a teenager:

> *"Your identity must never be in the things that*
> *compete for space in your heart. Don't diminish the*
> *price paid for you or minimize God's adoption of*
> *you."*
> *(My Suffering Has Not Defined Me, article on*
> *desiringgod.org, accessed 12/5/19)*

That makes it sound as if I've got it all figured out now. I don't. The struggle still remains. But as I've wrestled afresh with new losses and battled the desire to find my confidence, hope, and identity in lesser things, I've learned to pray often:

> *"The dearest idol I have known,*
> *Whate'er that idol be,*
> *Help me tear it from Thy throne,*
> *And worship only Thee."*
> *(William Cowper, O For a Closer Walk with God)*

That is a brave prayer to pray, but a good one—because we are redeemed by Christ, we are secure in Christ, and we are headed home to Christ. I can be confident that "he knows the way I take; when he has tried me, I shall come out as gold" (Job 23 v 10)—and so can you.

REFLECT

- What are you most likely to look for security in, other than Christ? If you lost that thing, would Jesus be enough for you?
- Are there ways in which you find your security or identity in your marriage? Are there ways in which you look outside of your marriage to find something to satisfy you or give you purpose? How does this affect your relationship?
- If you do see ways in which you find your security or identity in your marriage, or in things outside of your marriage, how would understanding your identity in Christ change: your priorities; how you spend your time; and how you view your spouse and marriage?
- (Together, if possible) Discuss your answers to the questions above—you may have insights about your husband/wife that they haven't noticed themselves. Then ask: What changes need to be made to realign our priorities and desires to live with Christ as the center of our life and marriage?

PRAY

Heavenly Father, I confess that I am quick to look for my security, confidence, identity, and happiness in many things other than you. I fear that I will lose myself if I lose certain things or abilities that I have found confidence and enjoyment in. Please forgive me for idolizing the gifts you have given rather than worshiping you above all else. Enable me to understand and be secure in my identity in you, and show me areas that I am tempted to run to instead of you. Strengthen our marriage, but protect us from looking to it for our main purpose and joy. Help me to enjoy the blessings and gifts you have given, but to hold loosely to them and seek my greatest joy in you. Amen.

For further meditation: John 15 v 5; Romans 12 v 2; Galatians 2 v 20; Philippians 1 v 6; Colossians 3 v 1-4.

Journaling

_____

_____

_____

_____

_____

_____

_____

_____

_____

_____

_____

_____

_____

_____

_____

_____

_____

_____

_____

_____

CHAPTER 15

When You Feel Alone in the Storm

*He has put my brothers far from me, and those
who knew me are wholly estranged from me. My
relatives have failed me, my close friends have
forgotten me. (Job 19 v 13-14)*

As I scanned the room, watching the smiling faces
and friendly exchanges, somehow the space around
me seemed to grow smaller. Though the room was full of
people I knew, somehow I felt completely unknown. *If
only people could see,* I thought. *If only they knew the deep
pain that is etched upon my heart.* Yet even if they could see,
what could they do? Somehow, amid all these people, I felt
incredibly alone.

Of course, I know that I'm not *truly* alone. I know that
Jesus lives within me, and I know that many people care
and do want to help. But the reality is that people, even
those with the best intentions, have a limited ability to
enter into someone else's pain. Even a spouse, who may
be walking through the same exact trial, is limited in their
understanding of how their husband or wife is uniquely
affected by it. Because of different temperaments, per-
sonalities, experiences, weaknesses, and levels of spiritual
maturity, no two people will suffer in exactly the same way,

nor will they perfectly understand each other's experience of their pain.

So how do we, as creatures created for relationship, navigate the dark corridors of loneliness? How do we not give way to the pull of loneliness, which tempts us to retreat and take up residence within the false comfort of our walls of isolation, with all the harm that such withdrawal will cause to our marriage?

REMEMBER...

First, we need to remember that, despite how lonely life can feel, we're not alone in the experience of loneliness. It's one of the most common human struggles, and has been since the beginning of time. Thankfully, God's word doesn't shy away from it. David cried out in Psalm 25 v 16-17, "Turn to me and be gracious to me, for I am lonely and afflicted. The troubles of my heart are enlarged; bring me out of my distresses." Jeremiah lamented in Lamentations 3 v 7-8, "He has walled me about so that I cannot escape; he has made my chains heavy; though I call and cry for help, he shuts out my prayer." And as we've seen, Job frequently mourned his lonely state: "He has put my brothers far from me, and those who knew me are wholly estranged from me. My relatives have failed me, my close friends have forgotten me" (Job 19 v 13-14).

Do you notice the common thread? Loneliness intensified in the affliction of all these people. So we shouldn't be surprised when it intensifies in ours as well. At times, our circumstances perpetuate a loneliness simply due to the nature of our trials (such as illness, or a child who has special needs) keeping us from the life we once knew. But often, loneliness finds its way into our hearts because our trials make us feel *different*. This is why we can be in a crowd of people and feel lonelier than when we're alone—we're carrying a weight that no one seems to see but us, and no one can fully understand but us.

BUILDING BRIDGES OR WALLS?

Because suffering has a way of distorting reality, we tend to make assumptions based upon our feelings and how things appear. Our eyes begin to paint the world with the colors of our feelings and perceptions. The more we live in this distorted reality—one that assumes that no one can understand or relate to our plight—the more we're tempted to isolate ourselves and sink deeper into our loneliness. It becomes a vicious cycle, and it takes an energy we feel we don't have to break out of it.

Within our marriage, too, our response to trials can be to build walls rather than bridges, creating a remoteness between spouses. On one hand, there is a depth and bonding that can come from walking through hardships alongside our husband or wife—the only other person who is as close to them as we are (other than God). But on the other hand, those very same hardships have the potential to isolate us from each other, so that our marriage becomes the most painful place of loneliness.

How do we move forward?

YOU ARE NOT THE ONLY ONE

God's word reminds us that suffering is not isolated to us. Not only is it simply part of living in this fallen world but we are promised that believers will all face various trials (though some will be greater than others). So loneliness shouldn't surprise us, nor is it an experience unique to us:

> *Beloved, do not be surprised at the fiery trial when it comes upon you to test you, as though something*

*strange were happening to you. But rejoice insofar as
you share Christ's sufferings, that you may also rejoice
and be glad when his glory is revealed.*
(1 Peter 4 v 12-13)

Because Jesus broke the curse of sin, trials (including loneliness) are no longer pointless or hopeless:

*In [hardships] you [can] rejoice, though now for a
little while, if necessary, you have been grieved by
various trials, so that the tested genuineness of your
faith—more precious than gold that perishes though
it is tested by fire—may be found to result in praise
and glory and honor at the revelation of Jesus Christ.*
(1 Peter 1 v 6-7)

As we come to realize that we are in the company of others
who are, perhaps unseen to us, also battling loneliness,
we can turn our focus off of ourselves and look to be the
friend we wish we had in others. We can steward the struggle by letting it make us more empathetic and quicker to
spot the outsider. Often, when we focus on being a friend
rather than wishing we had one, we end up being blessed in
return.

NOT UNDERSTANDING IS NOT THE SAME AS NOT CARING

Are you expecting something from others—including your
spouse—that they aren't able or meant to give? If we don't
allow our loneliness to drive us to Jesus, then inevitably we
will try to fill ourselves with what others can give us—and,
since no one else is your Savior, that will eventually leave
you hurt and disappointed. Since even we don't always
know what we need, it's no wonder that others don't either!
But Jesus does.

Loneliness increases not simply because we're alone but because we become fixated on people being the solution to our lonely state. That sets them up to fail us, and when they do we easily become bitter, resentful, needy, and withdrawn. Pastor Eric Geiger writes, "The more isolated you are, the more self-centered you are. And the more self-centered you are, the more likely you are to live isolated" (ericgeiger.com/2019/02/what-research-says-about-how-self-centeredness-grows-in-us, accessed 12/2/19). And the more isolated we are, the more vulnerable we are to being lured into the traps of sin and Satan's lies. It's no surprise, then, that Satan works extra hard to produce or perpetuate this isolation within our marriages, where the greatest damage can occur. Don't let him persuade you that your spouse should fully understand and always know what to say, and that since they don't, they don't really love you, and that is isn't worth the effort of seeking to communicate your struggles to them.

THE FRIEND WHO STICKS CLOSE

There is a better way: one that drives us into the all-satisfying comfort and presence of Christ (2 Corinthians 1 v 3b-5). Jesus is the only source of true comfort because not only is he the only one who can fully see, understand, and relate to our suffering, but he is the only one who has the power to comfort us in it and do something about it. Of course, he often uses people to bring his comfort, and friends and family can pray, bring a meal, and send notes of encouragement—but only Christ's Spirit can give us the strength to endure. The church can offer guidance, support, and encouragement from their limited understanding and wisdom, but only the "God of hope can fill you with all joy and peace in believing, so that by the power of the Holy Spirit you may abound in hope" (Romans 15 v 13).

When Jesus takes his proper place as our *source* of comfort, joy, and satisfaction, our expectations of others will find their proper place as well. God has given us the body of Christ and our marriages as blessings and his provision to enable us to serve and love one another out of the overflow of our satisfaction and joy in him.

So when Jesus becomes the source of our comfort and the answer to our loneliness, our response changes from demanding the constant comfort and perfect help of others to graciously receiving the imperfect offerings of others, and giving comfort to those around us. Amazingly, if loneliness drives us deeper into the comfort of Christ, it doesn't isolate us from others but instead it further motivates us to live in community with other believers (and most importantly with our spouse) with a genuine desire to give to others what we have received through the Spirit. Little by little, our loneliness begins to turn to joy, not because other people are meeting our needs and desires in the way we want them to, but because Christ has proved to be enough.

If you find yourself in a very lonely season, feeling abandoned by those around you, as Job did, remember that being alone or misunderstood doesn't need to equate with loneliness in the truest sense of the word. You have a Savior who was often alone, and who empathizes with you. The very solitude that trials often force upon you can bring you to know the nearness and presence of Jesus in a way you may never have known otherwise.

LANGUAGE FOR OUR LONELINESS

And when God, too, seems distant from us, we can find language for our feelings in the Scriptures. Job cried, "Behold,

I go forward, but he is not there, and backward, but I do not perceive him; on the left hand when he is working, I do not behold him; he turns to the right hand, but I do not see him" (Job 23 v 8-9). He knew the darkness and pain of circumstances that seemed to darken his view of God to the point that he questioned where God was.

For whatever reason, God sometimes seems silent. We struggle to feel his presence and comfort. Though I don't understand God's ways and I still deeply struggle with why he seems silent at times, I wonder if it's for the purpose of fanning the spark of faith within us—for giving us a greater hunger and longing for his presence. Like the psalmist, we can use his silence to plead for his nearness:

> As a deer pants for flowing streams,
>   so pants my soul for you, O God.
> My soul thirsts for God,
>   for the living God.
> When shall I come and appear before God?
> My tears have been my food
>   day and night,
> while they say to me all the day long,
>   "Where is your God?" (Psalm 42 v 1-3)

Loneliness does not need to extinguish hope. We need to counter our feelings with facts: and the fact is that Jesus bore the silence of God and the distance of God so that you and I never need to. "Neither death nor life, nor angels nor rulers, nor things present nor things to come, nor powers, nor height nor depth, nor anything else in all creation, will be able to separate us from the love of God in Christ Jesus our Lord" (Romans 8 v 38-39). That may not feel true, but it remains true. One day, there will no longer be any remnant left of the loneliness we often feel in this life. We will be in the presence of Jesus, seeing his face at last, never to be veiled again. Sin and suffering will be no more (Revelation 21 v 4)—oh, what a day that will be!

Until that day, fight back against loneliness by rehearsing what is true and stepping out in faith. If loneliness has settled into your marriage, make a conscious effort to move toward your spouse rather than shutting yourself off from them. You might need to be clear about what you need (for example, "I just need you to listen right now and not try to fix this"). Appreciate any desire in them to understand, rather than demanding or expecting a perfect response. And if loneliness has settled into your relationship with God, cry out to him, asking for a confidence that he is near when you do not feel it; and for him to be at work so that your feelings would come to reflect that truth. It's as you remember that Christ is never far from you that you are enabled to take down the walls within your marriage, and so you become able to receive the comfort and blessing of having one another to walk alongside through a season of trials.

REFLECT
- Do you struggle with loneliness (outside or within your marriage)? If so, when, and why? What truths from God's word can you rehearse to yourself in those moments?
- If you feel like God is distant, what truth have you learned in Job (and other places in God's word) that can remind you of what is true when you feel he is absent or silent?
- What practical steps can you take to push back against the suffocating walls of loneliness?
- (Together, if possible) Ask each other if you ever feel loneliness within your marriage, and when and why you think that is. Discuss if there are practical ways

to help each other when loneliness sets in. If you both struggle with loneliness because of your circumstances, how can you encourage each other to lean more into Christ in this season? Discuss ways to fight against the temptation to isolate yourself and lose perspective in your trials.

PRAY

Jesus, this life can feel so lonely. The harder life has become, the more I've been tempted to pull away from others in fear of being misunderstood or hurt by their words or silence. Even though I see people all around me, it feels like no one truly sees me—including, at times, my wife/husband. I know that, too often, my fear of loneliness has tempted me to fill that void with empty things and momentary distractions, rather than turning to you. Help me to trust that you will meet me with comfort and strength when I seek you. Forgive me for looking for my needs and desires to be met by other people and for being resentful when they aren't. Please use this time to draw me to yourself and help me trust that you can satisfy and meet the needs, desires, and longings of my heart in a way that no one else can. Jesus, don't be far off in my loneliness. Help me know the nearness, comfort, and joy of your presence. Amen.

For further meditation: Deuteronomy 31 v 6; 1 Samuel 12 v 22; Psalm 23 v 1-6; Lamentations 3 v 25-30; Romans 8 v 35-39.

Journaling

CHAPTER 16

Suffering and Intimacy (Part One)

"My breath is strange to my wife." (Job 19 v 17)

I admit, I've somewhat dreaded this chapter. Jeff, on the other hand, probably couldn't wait!

All joking aside, there is no area of our marriage that has involved more tears, more arguments, and more need of God's help than this one. The complexities and nuances of sex and intimacy are enough to write an entire book about. So we want to be clear—we don't have all the answers, and we will not be able to give a full picture of the importance or challenges of this aspect of married life. We are still (and probably always will be, to some degree) on our own marital journey. We are still tearing down distortions, working through past wounds, laying down our defenses, addressing wrong patterns of thinking, and learning to trust Christ to rebuild this area of our marriage with his truth at the center.

And we've talked to enough hurting couples to know that we're not the only ones struggling. In fact, many couples have expressed frustration over the lack of resources and discussion within their churches to address the struggles that many marriages face in regards to sex and intimacy. Of course, there has to be discretion in how and when this topic is discussed, but because of its sensitive and complicated nature, it's often avoided altogether. One of the reasons we wanted to (or needed to) include two chapters on intimacy in this book was because the majority of marriage books we've read (though I'm sure there are others out there) have mainly focused on the spiritual aspects of sexual intimacy between a husband and wife and fail to address the various nuances and challenges facing many marriages today. (Certainly, none of the ones we've read have used Job 19 v 17 to introduce the topic!) The reality is that when storms break over our marriage, they tend to affect what goes on in bed—and often it's what is (or isn't) happening in bed that causes the storms themselves. We may see how we want things to be, but at times our circumstances make that desire seem an impossible reality.

In the next two chapters, we will not focus as much on the biblical black and white reasons why sexual intimacy within a marriage (and only within a marriage) is important; instead, we will try to address intimacy as a whole and look at some of the gray areas that many couples are faced with. We won't have all the answers to these challenges, but our hope is to offer you some encouragement and prompt helpful conversation between you and your spouse.

You may notice that the word *intimacy* is used a lot throughout these next two chapters, and that's deliberate—because, while sex is a subset and expression of intimacy, what matters truly is an intimacy that flows throughout your marriage (and therefore, as part of that, helps you to enjoy your sex life together).

SEX IS NOT THE SAME AS INTIMACY

(Jeff) Sex and intimacy are not interchangeable. Two people can engage sexually but be completely detached from one another on every other level. Typically, at the beginning of our marriage, infatuation and sexual chemistry drive our

relationship—and we might assume that it will always be so. But over time, as the stressors of life press in and the excitement of infatuation begins to fade, we discover how much *intimacy* we really have. This is because sex and physical "closeness" is only one aspect of marital intimacy. Intimacy is about drawing close to every part of your spouse—emotionally, physically, intellectually, and spiritually.

We see this in Genesis 4 v 1, where it says, "Adam knew Eve his wife." That word "knew" describes sex, but it also carries a depth far beyond the act of sex. The marriage and family counselor Greg Smalley wrote:

> *"The word yada (to know) is a powerful image clarifying that sex doesn't just involve the body, but the heart and mind as well. The metaphor of sex as knowing is an important aspect of the term yada. It implies discovery, actively pursuing knowledge about your spouse. 1 Peter 3 v 7 says, 'Likewise, husbands, live with your wives in an understanding way.' Here, husbands are instructed to dwell with their wives according to knowledge. This type of knowing happens when we take on an attitude of curiosity and ask questions to better understand our spouse's emotions, fears, hopes, dreams, concerns, likes, dislikes, etc. I believe that one of the deepest human needs is to be known by our spouse—to experience intimacy. In slowing down the pronunciation of the word intimacy, we get something similar to 'into me see.' And that's where yada comes into the picture. Curiosity can create an emotional connection that's often a prerequisite for a woman to connect sexually with her husband."*
> *(Does "Yada, Yada, Yada" in Your Marriage Mean it's "Blah, Blah, Blah"? www.focusonthefamily.com, accessed 12/5/19)*

No one talks about this in church on a Sunday morning or at work on a Monday morning, but more couples than you'd guess face this struggle or disappointment.

We should view sexual intimacy as the overflow of intimacy from the rest of the marriage. Though God graciously designed sex to be enjoyed on a physical level, he also created it to mirror the mystery of Christ's love for his bride, the church (Ephesians 5 v 28-32). Sexual unity was designed to be an outward expression of love, respect, friendship, and trust between a husband and wife. It's what leads Solomon's bride in Song of Solomon to exclaim, "His mouth is most sweet, and he is altogether desirable. *This is my beloved and this is my friend"* (5 v 16, my emphasis).

So sex is not the defining point of our marriage—but it can be an indicator of the health of our marriage. Relational intimacy should fuel sexual intimacy, and sexual intimacy should fuel relational intimacy. The reason why this is important is because we often view sex as a compartmentalized part of the marriage, rather than something connected to the rest of the marital "body."

Some of you reading this, however, are likely feeling crushed by all of this. "That sounds great," you want to say (or shout, or cry), "but our sex life is a shambles, and I don't even know where to begin." If that's you, let me first assure you that you're not alone. No one talks about it in church on a Sunday morning or at work on a Monday morning, but more couples than you'd guess face struggle or regret or disappointment over their sex life together. Second, what seems impossible to you is never impossible to God. He really can do more than you ask or can even think of (Ephesians 3 v 20). Begin in prayer, for yourself and for your spouse, asking Christ to do what only he can do.

Third, even when we think the problem lies with our spouse, it's important that we evaluate ways that we may have gotten off track as well. All of us tend either to elevate sex as the primary purpose and desire of our marriage or to lower its value as an unnecessary optional aspect of it.

THE TOO-HIGH VIEW AND THE TOO-LOW VIEW

(Jeff) We live in a sex-saturated culture that gives the appearance that it greatly values it, when in reality we've only cheapened it. We drink the water we swim in, and so this atmosphere infiltrates our marriages in one way or another. As is true for any good gift from God, we can end up worshiping sex above Christ and valuing sex more than our spouse. Rather than viewing it as an act of vulnerable trust and selflessness in pursuit of intimacy with the one you love, it becomes a desire to be fulfilled and a right to be demanded. This idolizing of sex takes what God meant to unify us into one flesh (Genesis 2 v 24) and turns it into a loveless, self-serving transaction. Between the prevalence of pornography and the sexualization of everything (just watch a few commercials), it's no wonder that sex and intimacy have been distorted both in and out of marriage. This sexualization has promoted a culture of empty sex, sexual abuse, and spouses who feel used rather than cherished.

A spouse who expects and demands sex from their husband or wife, regardless of the cost to their spouse, is not pursuing the intimacy that God has designed for marriage. No matter how someone may try to rationalize it by misusing Scriptures such as 1 Peter 3 v 1 or 1 Corinthians 7 v 3-4, this attitude is harmful to your spouse, your marriage, and your own soul. Sadly, I believe there are far too many marriages within the church that are living with this dynamic, to the point where sexual abuse in "Christian marriages" has become increasingly prevalent but, unfortunately, is often ignored. If you are in a marriage where this is the case, please do not believe the lie that God commands you to submit to such behavior. It's sinful, wrong, and unbiblical. Please reach out for help and wisdom from a trustworthy Christian mentor or leader who has the ears to hear and doesn't brush it under the rug or make excuses for it. Lord willing, healing can come from even these broken relationships, but often that doesn't happen until drastic measures are taken to make room for such change.

As Ellen Dykas, who works for Harvest USA, says:

> *"God calls us to love our spouse selflessly. This means that the Bible never blesses non-consensual sexual expression/activity, or hurting, shaming, manipulating, or withholding to punish."*
> *(Personal Correspondence)*

If something doesn't reflect the way Christ loves his church, it should not be a part of a marriage. There is a huge difference between desiring sex—and looking to our spouse to fulfill that want—and desiring our *spouse*, with sexual intimacy being just one expression of that. I guarantee that your spouse will know the difference.

Brother and sister, we do need to ask: are we (and how are we) viewing sex through the distorted lens of the culture and our own sinful desires, elevating sex as the main pursuit of our marriage? Here is one way to help you answer: if a close friend asks how your marriage is going, would your answer be based on internally quantifying how much sex you've had recently, how good it was, and how often your desires are being met?

A healthy, biblical view of sex does not elevate sex above other aspects of marriage but sees it as a gauge that measures the temperature of the marriage and highlights any underlying issues that may be impacting intimacy and trust. A Christian who truly wants to please the Lord and love their spouse will pursue health in the whole marriage, and not purely for the sake of more sex. This includes *how* we engage in sexual relations with our spouse. Beware of a "too-high" view of sex.

(Sarah) On the flip side, we can also have too low a view of sex. Sometimes it's simply because one spouse has a much lower sex drive, which can be for many different reasons (hormonal, physical, mental, or emotional). For some, the lack of need or desire often intensifies in seasons of child-bearing—having children either in us, on us, or needing something from us nearly 24 hours a day does affect your sex drive. Between exhaustion, commitments, stress, chores, and a constant sense of "giving of ourselves" to our kids, at work, or—yes—in serving our church family, sex can sometimes feel like yet another area of sacrifice in our already depleted physical, emotional, and mental state.

Additionally, many people enter into marriage with sexual pasts that continue to impact them today. Our view of sexuality has often been shaped by our experience long before we were married—and those effects will inevitably seep into our relationship if they aren't addressed.

When we have less of a physical desire and face circumstances that often suck the life out of the desire that we do have, it can be tempting to devalue (or even detest) sexual intimacy in our marriage. When we do this, it is not just sex that we rob ourselves (and our spouse) of—it robs us of the full spectrum and depth of intimacy that God has designed us to experience and enjoy in our marriage.

However, it is important for us to realize that this full depth of intimacy will look different within every marriage. There is no "gold standard" to aim for, either in frequency or quality of sex (as our culture would define quality). It's freeing to realize that, biblically speaking, sex is part of a greater whole—the expression of love and commitment and vulnerability—that often comes more through times when the sex isn't "great" than when it's easy. In fact, it's possible to have a strong and happy marriage without the world's definition of good sex, and it's possible to have great sex (narrowly defined) in a toxic marriage. The first can satisfy and sanctify—the second can do neither.

In essence, sex or sexual intimacy is not meant to be the foundation or ultimate purpose of marriage, but it should be a highly valued aspect of a marriage built on trust, sacrifice, humility, friendship, love, and cherishing one another. Will a husband and wife always do this well? No. Will there be seasons when we may need prayerfully to seek wisdom, healing, and growth? Probably. Are there occasional circumstances that make the physical act of sex impossible? Yes. But when we value our marriage as God does and we seek to *know* all of our spouse, there will be a greater richness, depth, and enjoyment in our marriage—in and out of the bedroom.

And so, given the ebbs and flows we'll all face in this area, couples have to keep the lines of communication open. In an area where we are meant to be the closest, sometimes we're the furthest from each other—and the only way to bridge that divide is to be willing to have the hard conversations. If we are struggling but are still talking, then we're moving in a good direction. But if we shut down, won't communicate or express how we feel, and are unwilling to hear each other's perspectives, we will struggle to move forward—or worse, we'll move apart.

As sinners in the process of sanctification, this will always be a dance. Sometimes one spouse will put in more effort in certain areas, sometimes we'll step on each other's toes, sometimes we'll get frustrated with our spouse's lack of effort and desire, and sometimes we'll feel like getting off the dance floor altogether. But in his grace, God can use these frustrations to lead us both to dependence on Christ and a deeper love for our husband or wife. When we depend on him, he will gradually work in us a humble, sacrificial, patient, and loving desire to dance with our spouse in the way God created us to—for our joy and to reflect his glory. And what a beautiful dance it is.

REFLECT

- Do you view sex as a separate part of your marriage or as one aspect of intimacy within it? Do you tend to lean more in the direction of having too high a view or too low a view of sexual intimacy?
- In what ways are your motives for sexual intimacy coming from a heart of selfless love? Are there ways in which you act out of a desire to get what makes you feel good, regardless of how it makes your spouse feel?
- What part of this chapter did you find most helpful, either in encouraging or challenging you? Are there practical changes you need to make, or to discuss with your spouse?
- (Together, if possible) Discuss your sexual intimacy, and your intimacy more widely. Each ask the other: "How can I show you love in our sex life? Are there ways in which I am getting this wrong?" Listen to each other's answers without any interruptions or non-verbal responses. If you are not on the same page, then consider committing to pray for this area of your marriage on a regular basis, giving your expectations and desires to Christ, and asking him to help you love your spouse with his love.

PRAY

Lord, I want to be at a place where I am displaying sacrificial and selfless love, but sometimes I don't know where to begin or how to get there. Please give me an accurate view of what biblical sexual intimacy is and how we can grow in this area of our marriage. Soften my heart to put my needs and desires second and to look for ways to grow intimacy in all areas of our marriage. By your grace, give me pure motives so that I serve and love my spouse well and don't place too little or too much importance on the area of sexual intimacy. Restore and grow this part of our marriage to reflect your love and to bring greater unity between me and my husband/wife. Amen.

For further meditation: Psalm 107 v 9; Song of Solomon 5 v 16; Romans 12 v 10.

Journaling

_____

_____

_____

_____

_____

_____

_____

_____

_____

_____

_____

_____

_____

_____

_____

_____

_____

_____

_____

_____

_____

_____

CHAPTER 17

Suffering and Intimacy (Part Two)

"If you will start to see your spouse as God sees your spouse, if you will cultivate the affection God already has for the person to whom you're married, your relationship will never be the same."
(Gary Thomas, A Lifelong Love, page 33)

Gary Thomas' words, as they have worked their way into our hearts, have not only changed our marriage; they have helped us withstand and navigate nearly constant attacks against our pursuit of intimacy. It hasn't been easy, and we're still learning this dance, but God has used the challenges we've faced to center us in the gospel and gradually change our hearts toward each other.

There are many layers and challenges to the pursuit of intimacy, and this is a more practical (though, of course, hardly exhaustive) chapter, where we apply the wisdom that God has given to the situations we face in marriage. We've broken the challenges we face when it comes to sex into three separate categories of struggle: heart, physical, and emotional.

HEART ISSUES: *SELFISHNESS*

(Both) All of our heart issues stem from elevating ourselves above others (including God). Most of the battles we face

in regards to our sexual intimacy revolve around the issue of selfishness.

For example, we might think, "He hasn't been helping around the house, and now I'm exhausted because I had to pick up the slack, so he better not expect anything from me tonight." Or "We haven't been physical in a long time, so she can't blame me for looking at pornography." Selfishness often leads to either a too-high or too-low view of sex.

Self-serving attitudes are a sure-fire way to kill intimacy in our marriage. Why? Because intimacy is cultivated through a humble, sacrificial love that says, "I desire you for you, not because of what you can give me or do for me. I find joy in serving, loving, and respecting you in a way that reflects Christ's love. I want to know you more deeply as my friend, teammate, and love." Consider our relationship with God. He doesn't simply demand that we come to him; he beckons us with a love that flows from his own sacrifice. "I have loved you with an everlasting love; therefore I have drawn you with loving-kindness" (Jeremiah 31 v 3, NASB). Jesus draws us into his safe, loving, and satisfying arms, not because we deserve it but because he loved us enough to lay down his own life for our freedom and joy in him. That is the kind of love that leads to intimacy and resists the temptation to misuse sex.

ANGER/BITTERNESS

> *Be angry and do not sin; do not let the sun go down on your anger. (Ephesians 4 v 26).*

(*Jeff*) For men, our frustrations or anger toward our wives typically originate from feeling disrespected or that our needs or desires are not being met. While the desire to be physically close to our spouse is a God-given one, sometimes we're pursuing the act of sex rather than intimacy as a whole (a too-high view of sex). But brothers, there is more pleasure in *knowing* your wife than in just *having* your wife. You must pursue her heart before you pursue her body.

This doesn't mean, though, that we aren't to be honest with our wife. You may need to find a way gently to talk about how you're feeling rather than bottling it all up and letting it turn into anger. If there is no physical intimacy, then there is a problem, and you can be honest with your wife about your frustrations and disappointments rather than thinking you shouldn't feel them at all.

(Sarah) Men generally have the ability to compartmentalize their feelings, but women often can't. If a woman is feeling hurt or unappreciated, then anger and bitterness will hinder her in being vulnerable with her husband. Sisters, though it's easier to try to ignore these feelings, or even "give in" to your husband to avoid conflict, true intimacy will only come through humble honesty and communication. As you prayerfully examine and acknowledge the source of anger and bitterness, you may see that it stems from unrealistic expectations and pride that needs to be confessed to the Lord. At the same time, you need to be honest with your husband about what has been bothering you enough for your anger to blossom into bitterness. (And if you are feeling unsafe, or fearful, then you need to communicate that, too: either to your husband, or to someone else who you trust and who is qualified to help you.)

PRIORITIES
(Both) If intimacy (in any area) is lacking, it may simply be because it's not a priority (a too-low view of sex). We may need to ask ourselves if we are giving so much of ourselves in other areas that we're neglecting our spouse. There are seasons when more will be demanded of us (such as trying

to get a baby to sleep for more than two hours at a time or a heavy season of travel for work), but if this becomes the norm after these seasons pass, we may need to re-evaluate our priorities.

EXPECTATIONS

(Both) Expectations are the enemy of intimacy. If we expect something, we're looking for what we can get rather than what we can give. If you're struggling in this area, it's good to ask yourself if you are disappointed and frustrated with your spouse because you are expecting something from them that either they are unaware of or they aren't able to give. Expectations can, without us really noticing, become demands—and those are corrosive to the marriage as a whole.

PHYSICAL ISSUES: *CHRONIC OR MENTAL ILLNESS*

(Sarah) This is an area of struggle for many couples, but it's also one of those gray areas that isn't often talked about, and one that we have struggled with in our own marriage. Because my illness often causes me to feel achy, sick to my stomach, and depressed and anxious, it sometimes feels impossible to think of anything else. I've struggled both with guilt over not feeling well and irritation at having to push through the pain for the greater good of my marriage. Over the last couple of years, the Lord has graciously used this painful struggle to drive both of us to seek Christ for healing, wisdom, and provision. He has taught us to communicate more honestly, navigate what works best for us in our circumstances, and rely on him for the strength to love each other well.

Sometimes, there is a medical issue that inhibits performance or ability. While certain medical issues may be irreversible, there are particular ones for which we simply need to be willing to set aside our pride and seek medical help—just as we would for a broken leg. Though there isn't always a solution or easy answer, it's wise to use what God has given us (such as doctors and medicine) to improve our situation if it's possible.

If you are going through a season of pain or sickness right now that's preventing you and your spouse from being physically close, it will be important to look for other meaningful ways to show that you're thinking of your spouse and have the desire to be physically intimate with them, even though your current state is preventing it today. Sharing your sincere desire can help prevent the false assumption that physical intimacy is unimportant to you. Rather than retreating in guilt, embarrassment, or frustration, being honest with your spouse about the struggle will guard against creating walls built on false assumptions.

This struggle can be incredibly straining on a marriage. But personally, what has drawn me toward Jeff and grown my love and respect for him has been the ways he has communicated that he will not abandon me and that his love for me will not change if our sexual intimacy can't be exactly as he desires it to be. At times, God may call a husband or wife to a greater level of sacrifice because of the illness of their spouse—at that point it's crucial to fight a too-high view of sex and remember that there is blessing to be found in laying down our own "life" for a friend, just as our Lord did (John 15 v 13; 13 v 14).

PAINFUL INTERCOURSE

(Both) This is another struggle that many couples have but often don't talk about due to embarrassment or shame. Sometimes, for medical reasons, a woman experiences excruciating pain in sex. This often produces guilt for her husband, who feels he has pleasure at the cost of his wife's pain. Meanwhile the wife can vacillate between guilt over the disappointment her pain causes and frustration over giving herself in a way that is painful and far from enjoyable. Again, there are no easy answers to this. The Bible does not require us to give of ourselves in a way that causes pain; but love in this context would also not look like retreating from the issue by not having sex and ignoring the problem. Couples should seek medical guidance along with wise godly counsel. Some of the most helpful advice we have received is that intercourse is not the only means of sexual intimacy and we may need to think more creatively in how we connect physically. If God has allowed a struggle in our lives, he promises to provide what we need to navigate it: "Let us then with confidence draw near to the throne of grace, that we may receive mercy and find grace to help in time of need" (Hebrews 4 v 16).

EMOTIONAL ISSUES: *PAST ABUSE*

(*Sarah*) For many years in our marriage, I would have an involuntary reaction of shaking whenever I was touched. No matter how hard I tried to change, my body would react out of a deeply ingrained sense of self-protection as a result of past abuse. I was only further confused, hurt, and terrified by knowing what God's word says about how I should be using my body to serve and please my husband, as he used his to serve me. I couldn't help but view those Scriptures through the distorted perspective of my experience, leading me to devalue sex further. Overcoming this has taken years of counsel, both individually and alongside Jeff, and years of prayer for God to do a profound work of healing. I'm so thankful that this deep pain of my past didn't destroy our marriage as it could have, and that God has used the brokenness of it to draw us both closer to Christ and each other. It's been harder than I ever could have imagined, but it hasn't been wasted.

If you can relate to the effects of past abuse or harassment, I'm so very sorry. As painful as it is, I hope you will be able to talk to your spouse, and to your God, about it. Though it may feel impossible, I want to encourage you to see that there is great hope for those who seek God's help and rely on his power to work in their lives. I'd also encourage you to spend time using the language of lament, offered to us through Job and the Psalms, bringing all of your pain and past hurts to Christ. Know that God grieves with you and trust that he is able to bring you comfort and healing. It may not be quick, and it will not be easy, but there is hope for healing and res-toration. Through godly and wise counsel, time and patience, and the help of the Holy Spirit, your marriage can grow to experience the blessing of safe, healthy, and trust-filled inti-macy. Your Savior never demeans, abuses, or causes shame. And he is able to help.

FEELING UNLOVED OR DISRESPECTED
(Both) We've talked about this elsewhere, but it's worth saying again because it's so easy to get it wrong without even noticing it. Husbands, if you want your wife to desire to be close to you physically, she needs to know that you desire all of her, not just her body. Seek to know her desires, fears, burdens, and interests. Make her feel cherished because she is your bride, not just so that you can get something out of her. Wives, remember that although you may not be wired the same way as your husband, although the world has dis-torted sexuality, and although you may have been hurt in the past, God has created your husband to feel honored and respected when you desire him physically and show him your love in a way that expresses a desire to know all of him.

But honoring and respecting them begins long before sex; it begins in our thought life and is lived out in our actions.

UNFAITHFULNESS

(Both) Unfaithfulness is any form of emotional or physical intimacy with someone other than our spouse. Seeds of unfaithfulness can be planted in subtle ways, whether through reading or watching graphic romance novels or movies, confiding in a friend or coworker more than in our spouse, or finding physical pleasure apart from our husband or wife. The seeds grow if we do not destroy them when they first appear. They grow quickest in the soil of the lie that we "deserve" intimacy somewhere if we are not finding it at home. Unfaithfulness is never harmless. We are dishonoring God and our spouse, and we are stealing from them (and ourselves) the blessings God gives in the intimacy and trust that grows within lifelong, unconditional commitment.

It may be accepted by our culture, but one of the most prevalent forms of unfaithfulness today is the use of pornography. It feeds on our desire for intimacy but offers it in a way that promises immediate reward with no cost to ourselves. However, the cost is disastrous to our marriage and our own souls. It exchanges real intimacy for cheap, empty, self-serving pleasure.

The challenges of picking up the pieces after unfaithfulness are lengthy and difficult. Even if there is repentance and a willingness from both parties to embark on the long road of healing and restoration (which can only come through Christ), physical intimacy will only be possible through a commitment to rebuild trust over time, usually requiring godly counsel and support. Though God can, and has, restored many marriages after unfaithfulness, it won't happen unless sin is acknowledged, repented of, and turned away from.

If you have experienced unfaithfulness in your marriage, by God's grace, healing is possible if you're both willing. Don't let Satan tell you that even if there is repentance, there can never be a future for your marriage. God is a God of redemption and delights in bringing himself glory through seemingly impossible situations. Though restoration is not guaranteed, it is not impossible.

LACK OF TRUST

(Both) Intimacy flows from trust. If someone doesn't believe they are safe (physically or emotionally) with their husband or wife, they will be unwilling to let their guard down— and intimacy will suffer. If your spouse is withdrawn and unwilling to be intimate, ask them if there is anything that's fueling a lack of trust. It may simply be a misunderstanding, but often it reveals deeper issues that to be addressed. If trust has been broken, it won't be restored overnight, especially when wounds run deep. It will take time to build it back up, but God is faithful to those who hope in him.

Brother, sister, most of us will relate to one or more of these struggles and see how they affect our pursuit of intimacy in our marriages. But here's the good news—none of these struggles fall outside of God's ability to bring change and renewal. You don't have to have it all figured out. You do need to acknowledge the struggles and be willing to ask for his strength and wisdom to take the next step. You can gradually move toward greater intimacy with your spouse as you navigate these trials with the grace and wisdom that only Christ can provide. Be encouraged: no marriage is beyond his help, and no intimacy is so broken that it cannot be restored. After all, he is the God "who gives life to the dead and calls into existence the things that do not exist" (Romans 4 v 17).

REFLECT

- Which one (or more) of these challenges have you faced (or are you facing) in your marriage?
- If you are dealing with a struggle that affects sexual intimacy in your marriage, do you believe that God can bring healing to that area, and if he doesn't, that he can still provide a way for you to enjoy intimacy in a creative way?
- (Together, if possible) With sensitivity, try to be honest with each other about the challenges you are facing and share your desires, fears, concerns, and disappointments. If you're not in a place to do this, write these down individually and use them to pray about those things to the Lord. If your spouse is willing, discuss one or two practical steps you can take to grow in this area and make the best out of the challenges you are up against.

PRAY

Lord, I desire to have sexual intimacy in my marriage (or I want to desire it), but there is so much going against us. Please help us navigate the challenges we face together and be willing to be honest about the struggles. I find it easy to focus on how I wish things were; please show me how to walk alongside my wife/ husband faithfully through the storms we face. Help us to love each other well in this area and pursue intimacy in whatever capacity we are able to. Protect us from the enemy's attempts to divide us, and give us the strength, wisdom, and willingness to grow in all areas of intimacy—even if that looks different than we imagined it would. And however things go from here, make me faithful in my marriage, hopeful for change, and committed to showing the same selfless love that you have poured out on me. Amen.

For further meditation: Psalm 103 v 1-5; 1 Corinthians 13 v 4-8; Philippians 2 v 3-10; Philippians 4 v 11-12, 19.

Journaling

CHAPTER 18

Longing for Kids, Struggling with Kids: When Family Isn't What You Dreamed Of

While he was yet speaking, there came another and said, "Your sons and daughters were eating and drinking wine in their oldest brother's house, and behold, a great wind came across the wilderness and struck the four corners of the house, and it fell upon the young people, and they are dead, and I alone have escaped to tell you." (Job 1 v 18-19)

My dear friend sat across from me at our kitchen table. Despite the sun illuminating the room, a heaviness had settled upon both of us. Only eight months prior, we had shared in the excitement of finding out that we were both pregnant, our due dates just days apart.

Then, weeks later, the shadow fell. My friend and her husband were informed that their precious child would most likely only live a few days, if any. I wrestled with guilt over the unfairness of having a healthy child growing within me while she prepared for the loss of hers. But at the same time the pain of her loss resonated with me, because I had already endured year upon year of watching my hopes and expectations for parenthood slowly being stripped away through the pain of my kids' special needs and chronic illness.

Now here we were, after months of grieving, trusting, growing, and praying for God's intervention in each of our circumstances, discussing the likelihood of what—if there were to be no miracle—lay ahead. We were both struggling to come to grips with the deep ache of our dreams of what parenthood would be like disappearing—and with my friend's hopes for the future and her joy at watching her child grow suddenly being stripped away from her.

"Where is God?" we wondered. "If he is good, why is he allowing so much pain when we are seeking to follow him? Why won't he heal our children when we know that he can? How can we go on in life when these losses leave such gaping holes within our hearts? How do we navigate this road with spouses who are handling their stress and grief differently than us?"

These questions of faith (and emotions of an intensity we never thought we could feel) often come when you face grief over children: whether it is a longed-for child you could not have, a child you had and lost, or a child whose struggles have stripped away your dreams of parenting. We don't pretend to begin to understand every type of pain and grief that couples experience in this area of life. Yours may be far deeper than ours. But we do know the pain of the loss of the life with children that we once imagined; the fear of the future; the weight of being utterly unable to bring about what we most want to happen. Personally, we have found comfort in specific truths as we've struggled. So, while we don't know all the intricacies of the particular road you have walked, we pray that the God who does know all things will comfort your hearts as you read on.

WE HAVE PERMISSION TO GRIEVE

Relationships can be some of the sweetest gifts that we experience on this earth. But the sweetest gifts also cause the greatest pain when lost or broken. Children are a precious gift from the Lord (Psalm 127 v 3) and an incredible source of joy, but anyone who has lost a child, endured infertility, or watched their child suffer or cause suffering knows a pain that penetrates the deepest parts and can overwhelm us.

Job experienced it. Every one of his children was gone in an instant. Can you imagine the magnitude of such loss all in a moment? Some of you, tragically, can relate to this all too well. We see no response from Job after any of the previous catastrophes, but at the report of losing his children, he immediately responds in grief and mourning (Job 1 v 20). It's hard to fathom the agony he must have endured, unless you've been touched by a similar loss.

I'm so thankful that the Bible doesn't skirt around the deeply painful realities of living in a fallen world; rather, it addresses them head on. The book of Job not only shows us the many layers to suffering, but its length tells us that there are no easy answers, and we should beware of band-aid solutions to deep pain. Sometimes, a resolution doesn't ever come in this lifetime. Sure, someone could say, "Well, Job did end up having a resolution; in the end, he was blessed with even more prosperity than before, including ten more children!" (Job 42 v 13). But though I imagine Job must have found joy in those children, the ten he lost were still gone. Some things can never be replaced in our lifetime.

God's word shows us that we are not expected to move beyond grief to joy or leave loss behind and feel gratitude in one fell swoop—or ever. It's why so much of Job (along with Psalms and Lamentations) is filled with lament, teaching us the "honest cry of a hurting heart wrestling with the paradox of pain and the promise of God's goodness" (Mark

Vroegop, *Dark Clouds, Deep Mercy,* page 26). A Christian counselor shared an image with me that is helpful in this context: dealing with loss as a Christian is like traveling along an upward spiral. We move forward slowly, gradually moving past the initial pain and shock of loss, only to feel as though we've slid backwards yet again. For the parent who has lost a child, grief may continue to hit them years down the road, sometimes when they least expect it to surface. For someone struggling through years of infertility, there's the tinge of envy or surge of anger when a friend announces that they're having another baby while they themselves face disappointment month after month. For others, it may be in the constant reminders of what's been lost as they navigate the weariness, stress, and ongoing challenges of raising a child with special needs.

Over time, it's so easy to become discouraged and frustrated each time we slide back. But in reality, if the Holy Spirit lives in us, we've likely grown in ways that are difficult to discern when grief has struck a fresh blow upon our hearts.

When it comes to grief over kids, we learn to live with it, and because we have Christ, we can learn to have joy despite it—but we may never "get over it," and that's ok. As I've heard many people describe it, the losses we experience in regards to our children can feel like losing a limb. Part of yourself is gone, never to be fully restored on this earth. Eventually, you learn to live in that reality, learning how to function with one less limb, even experiencing joy again. But you will be forever aware of the loss, and of how you've been changed by it.

JESUS GRIEVES WITH US

We are rarely told how Jesus feels in the New Testament, so we should be impacted by it when we are. Notably, many of the passages that speak of Christ's emotions are highlighting his response to the needs, pain, or grief of others. On three separate occasions, when Jesus saw the multitude of crowds, he "had compassion on them"—the Greek work there, *splanchnizomai*, literally translates as "his guts churned" (Matthew 9 v 36; 14 v 14; and 15 v 32). Similarly, the Bible records that Jesus "had pity on" the two blind men in Matthew 20 v 34 and the leper in Mark 1 v 41; and again, the Lord "had compassion on" the widow of Nain whose son had just died, in Luke 7 v 13.

I don't know about you, but I find it comforting to know that Jesus, the God of all comfort, knows the kind of pain that makes your guts churn—that ache that is so deep that you feel it in the core of your being. Jesus felt that gut-wrenching compassion and pity not only for those who were lost and in need of a Savior, but in response to the pain and suffering of those he loved. Though he was fully God, his humanity meant he felt the depth of human emotion. The account of Lazarus shows us this paradox; despite Jesus knowing that Lazarus would be raised back to life, he was still so deeply moved and troubled by Mary's grief that he wept (John 11 v 33).

This makes a difference. Jesus not only cares about our grief; he grieves with us. As Joni Eareckson Tada wrote, sometimes "God permits what he hates to accomplish what he loves" (*When God Weeps*, page 84). His perfect love sometimes allows what he hates in order to accomplish his good purposes in our lives, for his glory and our eternal joy in his presence.

Jesus doesn't expect us to "get over it and just trust him." But he does want our grief and loss to draw us to him as we acknowledge and lament our losses, leaning on his grace to carry us through one moment at a time. As we do this, he gradually leads us to a place where we come to know grief and joy simultaneously. Romans 5 v 2-5 shows us this work of the Spirit:

> *Through him we have also obtained access by faith into this grace in which we stand, and we rejoice in hope of the glory of God. Not only that, but we rejoice in our sufferings, knowing that suffering produces endurance, and endurance produces character, and character produces hope, and hope does not put us to shame, because God's love has been poured into our hearts through the Holy Spirit who has been given to us.*

Today, you may feel a long way from being able to see or know anything beyond the crushing weight of grief. Jesus sees you, and he weeps with you. But keep talking to him, keep pouring your heart out to him, and keep reminding yourself that he knows the pain you feel—and he will walk with you through it.

One day at a time, as we look to the comfort of Christ to carry our grief and strengthen us, faithful endurance in the Spirit's strength gradually conforms us to the image of Christ. As we see glimmers of the Holy Spirit's work within us, even amidst continued grief, hope begins to grow and, somehow, the fruit of joy sprouts forth in the unexpected and undesired soil of suffering.

LOSS DOESN'T HAVE TO DIVIDE YOUR MARRIAGE

Kids make marriage harder. But frustrated hopes and shattered dreams when it comes to kids put our marriages under real pressure and can drive spouses apart. Yet it's also the case that the hardest moments in a marriage—and hard moments involving kids are often the hardest—are the moments when

Somehow, the fruit
of joy can sprout
forth in the unexpected
and undesired soil
of suffering.

as a couple we can draw together, and learn to love and trust each other more deeply. It's important to realize this, and to resolve prayerfully to let the pressure push you together rather than drive you apart.

We need to be willing to fight through what's difficult and to plod forward through the uncharted path of unchosen terrain together. And, as we discussed in chapter 3, we need to remember that the pain of loss often provokes very different responses in each of us. In a similar sense to our own "loss of a limb," we need to remember that our spouse has been changed as well. They may never be exactly the same person that they were before grief took up residence. Therefore we need to be patient and gracious with one another, recognizing that we each need time (at different levels and at different stages of processing the layers of loss) to learn how to live in our new reality. We need to keep talking, share about where we are struggling, discuss the spiritual questions that we currently wrestle with, and, most importantly, pray together (if our spouse is willing). There is something incredibly unifying when we come together in our weakness, lamenting and calling on the Lord's strength and comfort. It doesn't mean we will no longer lash out at each other from time to time or misunderstand and grow impatient now and then, but it will guard us from isolating ourselves and resenting each other for our differences along the way.

AT THE KITCHEN TABLE

In the end, what did my friend and I need most as we sat in my kitchen, and onwards during the hard months and years that followed, as our different struggles continued? We needed to grieve, as God encourages us to. We needed permission to need time, and to find the path hard, and God gives us that. We needed to know that Jesus understands and weeps with us, and the Scriptures show us that he does. And we needed to turn toward our spouses, and fight through together, and we encouraged each other to do that.

Though this is not the soil we ever would have chosen, God can take what could have destroyed us and use it to gradually bring forth new growth and renewed hope within our hearts and marriages—for his glory and our eternal joy.

REFLECT

- If you have experienced the loss of a child, an unmet longing for a child, a child with special needs, or a wayward child, what will it look like for you to bring your grief and hurt and fears before the Lord in honesty—perhaps for the first time—and then trust that he grieves with you and offers you comfort, strength, and the grace to carry you through each moment?

- How have losses or struggles in regards to children impacted your marriage? Has it grown you closer to each other or driven you apart? If it's driven you apart, why do you think that is? What small steps can you take that will enable you to start to grow closer?

- (Together, if possible) Discuss how challenges with children (or the desire or loss you've experienced) have either strengthened your marriage or driven you apart. Have you handled your grief or coped with the stress differently? Share ways in which you would like support from each other. Seeing how this struggle is impacting each of you may help you to be more compassionate to the other and to remember that you're on the same side, even if you're responding differently.

PRAY

Lord Jesus, this isn't how I imagined my life would go. The loss of anything is painful, but suffering loss in a way that touches my children (or the children I desire) sometimes feels like more than I can bear. I believe you are good, but this often doesn't feel good. I believe you are in control, but I struggle to understand why you allow the things that hurt so deeply. I believe you are faithful, but sometimes it's hard to see your faithfulness through the heartache. Jesus, help me trust that you love my child(ren) even more than I ever could, and if you withhold what I desire for them (or withhold our ability to have children), that you will somehow carry us through and satisfy the empty, hurting places of our hearts. Thank you that you weep when we weep. Thank you that you see, know, and feel my pain, disappointments, fears, and longings—and that you are able to meet me there. Give me the grace and strength for today to walk faithfully in the circumstances that you have allowed. Thank you that one day what is lost will be restored, what is broken will be made whole, and what is longed for will be fully satisfied. Amen.

For further meditation: Genesis 22 v 1-19; Psalm 34 v 17-20; John 9 v 1-3; 2 Corinthians 4 v 16-18; Revelation 21 v 4.

Journaling

_____

_____

_____

_____

_____

_____

_____

_____

_____

_____

_____

_____

_____

_____

_____

_____

_____

_____

_____

_____

CHAPTER 19

Why *Our* Family?

Why do the wicked live, reach old age, and grow
mighty in power? Their offspring are established in
their presence, and their descendants before their
eyes. Their houses are safe from fear, and no rod of
God is upon them. (Job 21 v 7-9)

As Sarah held our three-year-old's hand, his screams
pierced my heart as he fought the nurse's attempts to
insert a PICC line for his upcoming IV treatments. His
eyes were crying out to me for help. I just wanted to rescue
him, to make it stop. "I don't know if I can do this again,"
I thought, as the realization hit me that we would have to
go through this process three more times this week with
our other children.

I never wanted this for my children. In fact, I feared this
for my children. All I wanted was to provide for them a
normal childhood and to protect them from the hard realities
of living in this fallen world as long as I could. I have wrestled with how to process my desire to protect my children
from the things that God has chosen to allow. I've struggled
with how hard a road they've had to walk while many of
their young friends go on living a healthy, relatively pain-free
childhood. What do our children hear when we tell them
God loves them, when that love has not provided a pain-
free, healthy childhood? It's hard enough for us to navigate

suffering as mature believers, so how will they endure suffering in such profound ways at such young ages?

At times, it's tempting for me to look at other families (especially those who aren't following the Lord) whose children appear to be in perfect health and whose lives seem to be filled with comfort and ease, and ask myself—and God—"Why do we face all this hardship, while their lives seem untouched by pain?"

Job would have recognized this internal struggle, wondering why the lives of others (especially those of the wicked) appear free from struggle, their children flourishing and their houses free from fear: "no rod of God is upon them" (21 v 9). Though his perspective may not have been fully accurate, he sums up my thought process.

And yet… as much as we still struggle with those thoughts from time to time, God has increasingly shown us that our children's trials are not a sign of his disfavor. In fact, they may prove to be his grace at work in their lives.

THE FIRES CAN REFINE

What if the very things we fear for our children—and try to meticulously control and determinedly steer them away from—turn out to be the avenues that God will use to open their eyes to him? What if God uses the hardest of days (the ones we tried to avoid) to give them faith, grow their character, and set them on a different (yet eternally rewarding) path than we would have chosen for them? Consider the psalmist's words in Psalm 66 v 10-12:

> *For you, O God, have tested us;*
>   *you have tried us as silver is tried.*
> *You brought us into the net;*
>   *you laid a crushing burden on our backs;*
> *you let men ride over our heads;*

we went through fire and through water;
yet you have brought us out to a place of abundance.

I need to ask myself, "What do I honestly want more for each of my kids: a happy marriage, a great job, a long, pain-free, healthy life, their own kids, and so on—or faith in Christ and none (or only some) of those things?" Not only is this a hard question for each of us to answer, but it's an even harder one to live out in our parenting. If we're honest, we naturally want to protect our children from any pain or struggle, and so we can parent them in a way that shows we are more concerned for their temporary comfort and happiness than allowing God room to work in their lives as he sees best.

If you are walking a hard road with your child, or are gripped with fear over something that might threaten their comfort and happiness, I'd like to encourage you with some ways that I have seen God use suffering in the lives of our children and our family. He has worked in us in ways that I wouldn't change even if I could. My children have been touched by the Refiner's fire and are learning precious lessons in the midst of it.

KIDS CAN LEARN TO ENDURE

We don't have to live long to realize that life is hard, and if our children are to follow Christ, it won't be comfortable and pain-free. "We must go through many hardships to enter the kingdom of God" (Acts 14 v 22, NIV). But many of us live in a culture where children are catered to, cushioned, and overprotected, often producing entitled, overly anxious, self-absorbed, and fearful kids—and adults.

Should we do our best to protect our kids from obvious dangers? Yes, of course. But we also need to be careful that we aren't putting ourselves in the place of God, trying to control everything around them while thinking that we're doing them a service by preventing hardship and discomfort from entering their lives. We may be trying to protect them from the very things that will equip them to follow hard after Christ.

Although I would never have chosen for our children to be born into sickness and struggle, I have seen how God has used this suffering to teach them to seek him, do hard things, learn to endure, and grow in character along the way (James 1 v 3-4).

KIDS CAN LEARN TO LOOK FOR GOD'S FAITHFULNESS

We live in a Christian culture that is soaked in prosperity-gospel teaching and thinking—the idea that following Christ guarantees us health, wealth, and happiness on this earth. Many of us would probably be quick to decry that way of thinking, and yet we sometimes unknowingly and subtly believe a more "Reformed" version of that same false gospel. Most of us assume our day should go well—the car will start, the kids will be ok, our work will be successful, the TV will work, and so on. So when our plans are interrupted, or our health declines, or we lose our job, our response often reveals a belief that we think we deserve better.

Our kids' illnesses mean that there's no danger of them subconsciously growing up with the idea that faith buys comfort. They are experiencing first-hand that God is always faithful, but not always in the way we expect. As Lamentations 3 v 22-23 says, "The steadfast love of the LORD never ceases; his mercies never come to an end; they are new every morning; great is your faithfulness." Often, his steadfast love and faithfulness doesn't mean removing our pain but rather giving us his strength and provision through it. Our children have had a front-row seat to watch God provide financially for our family in seasons of desperate need. They have experienced the sweet provision of God when gifts were dropped off anonymously on our front step during Christmas time, and when meals have been consistently delivered from our church family.

While they have cried out in their frustration about the pain, they are also learning that Jesus sees their tears and answers their prayers—even if differently than they expect or desire. They are seeing that God's timetable and ways are different than their own. They have learned to be grateful for the small things and to appreciate blessings they would never have appreciated had they not experienced so much loss.

Of course, our children still throw tantrums, wish to be normal, and act like typical kids, but as they've experienced God's faithfulness in tangible ways, his presence and provision in the trials have gradually become sweeter.

KIDS CAN LEARN THAT SIN IS WORSE THAN PAIN

Pain has a way of tearing down our pretenses and our ability to mask our sin. For my kids and Sarah, it's physical pain. For me, it's the pain of being helpless to help those I love the most. And the awful truth is that when I watch them suffer and I feel helpless, I'm much quicker to snap at them, to complain about all the added responsibilities that I have to carry, and to blame everyone else for my responses. The pain doesn't cause my sin; it reveals my sin. The author Paul Tripp writes:

> *"You never just suffer the thing that you're suffering, but you always also suffer the way that you're suffering that thing … Your suffering is more powerfully shaped by what's in your heart than by what's in your body or in the world around you."*
>
> *(Suffering, page 27, 31)*

In other words, the outward pain we experience is only one aspect to our suffering. How we respond to our suffering—the idols that are revealed and the sin that is drawn to the surface—intensify the heat of the fire. But that is God's good purpose in our suffering: it comes "so that the tested genuineness of your faith—more precious than gold that perishes though it is tested by fire—may be found to result in praise and glory and honor at the revelation of Jesus Christ" (1 Peter 1 v 7).

As our family has endured years of trials, with no resolution or end in sight, God has helped us see that suffering is not really our main problem—sin is. This is not a pretty process, but it's been a good one, for all of us. Rather than living their childhood free from pain and ignorant of how deeply sin runs within them, God has used our children's trials to strip away the illusive veneer of triviality, revealing their need for a Savior.

As the psalmist wrote in Psalm 119:

> *Before I was afflicted I went astray*
> *but now I keep your word ...*
> *It is good for me that I was afflicted,*
> *that I might learn your statutes.*
> *The law of your mouth is better to me*
> *than thousands of gold and silver pieces.*
>
> *(v 67, 71-72)*

What a blessing it is as a Christian parent to see your children begin to grasp that Jesus is the greatest gift and that the pain they experience now is only temporary because they have the hope of eternity. Though I don't know for certain the state of each of my children's hearts, I'm thankful that God is providing many opportunities to sow seeds of the gospel in the soil of their souls.

WE WILL NOT FEAR

In Matt Chandler's book, *Joy in the Sorrow*, Jeanne Damoff shares a powerful testimony of God's faithfulness after her 15-year-old son was found at the bottom of a lake during a swimming party. Miraculously and against all medical prognoses, he gradually awoke from his coma and regained his ability to walk and talk and experience a joyful faith in Christ. Yet, as Jeanne shares, "His brain injury limits him to a very simple, dependent life. He'll probably never marry. Never have his own home or a real job. Never experience most of the things the world associates with success."

She then goes on to share her experience of joy in the sorrow as she grieved for her son:

> *"One day when sadness had swamped me yet again, I asked God to help me understand how this could be his will for Jacob. Then I felt like he asked me a question: What is your prayer for your children?*
>
> *"I said: 'When they stand in your presence, I want them to hear you say, "Well done, good and faithful servant."'*
>
> *"And it was as though God said, 'Look at him. He loves me with all his heart, and everyone who sees him is drawn to me. He is my faithful servant.'*
>
> *"What does it matter that Jacob will never impress the world with his accomplishments? He delights the One who created him for his own pleasure and glory, and his life is a shining portrait of redemption. What more could I ask for my son?"*
>
> *(pages 36-37)*

Truly, the greatest good for our children is to know and love Jesus beyond anything in this world. And sometimes it will take our child losing some of this world in order to motivate them to seek something (or Someone) beyond it.

Christian, if you are currently watching your child face hardship of some kind, remember that God loves your children more than you ever could, and he is trustworthy. There is so much to fear in this world, but when you come to fear and trust God more than you fear pain or trust your ability to control life, you will find greater freedom and peace in your parenting. Let's be parents who not only pray for the protection of our children but, first and foremost, pray that their hearts would turn to Christ, no matter the cost.

REFLECT

- Do you live in fear and anxiety over something happening to your child? If so, how would your parenting change if you took those fears and anxieties to the Lord instead, asking him to help you entrust your children into his trustworthy hands?
- Have you seen ways that hardship or disappointment has matured your son or daughter? How can that encourage you to pray positively, for growing faith and godliness, rather than only for an end to the pain or the trial?
- (Together, if possible) Discuss how you can support each other in this season, and how you can ensure that you are parenting consistently in how you treat your child(ren) and what you say to them.

PRAY

Heavenly Father, thank you that you promise to equip us for everything you call us to, even if that means you allow pain to enter our child's life. As a parent, my natural inclination is to protect my child from the pain and suffering of this world. Forgive me for times when I try to control their surroundings, rather than entrusting their life into your hands. Help me to know how to guard, teach, and protect my child in a way that honors you, but also to know when I need to step back and trust that you have a plan in allowing things beyond our control. Lord, please don't allow any pain in my child's life that will not be used to draw them to you and to give them life in your name. Give us the grace and wisdom to walk alongside them and parent them in a way that trusts and glorifies you. Amen.

For further meditation: Genesis 50 v 20; Isaiah 41 v 10; Isaiah 43 v 2; Jeremiah 17 v 7-8; Romans 5 v 3-5.

Journaling

_____

_____

_____

_____

_____

_____

_____

_____

_____

_____

_____

_____

_____

_____

_____

_____

_____

_____

_____

_____

CHAPTER 20

Prayers for Prodigal Children

Job would ... rise early in the morning and offer burnt offerings according to the number of them [his children]. For Job said, "It may be that my children have sinned, and cursed God in their hearts." Thus Job did continually. (Job 1 v 5)

Most parents feel the weighty responsibility of protecting and providing for their children, but Christian parents carry a burden that is far heavier than the fear of a broken arm or a broken heart. Being a Christian parent opens us up to the emotional toll and heartache of a child who rejects that which we hold most dear and know they most need—saving faith in Jesus Christ. It's the very reason that Job prayed for his children continuously, knowing their eternal salvation was at stake.

Yet as we all come to find out at one point or another, we can guide our children's lives, but we can't control their hearts. Job offered burnt-offering sacrifices for his children, revealing his urgent desire that they would be forgiven and live in relationship with God. But truly, each child has to decide for themselves whether or not they will trust in the sacrifice that all Old Testament burnt offerings pointed

I was once a "prodigal" child – lost and angry, hardened on the outside but deeply hurting within.

toward—Jesus, who "offered for all time a single sacrifice for sins" (Hebrews 10 v 12).

No matter what parenting manual we follow (or don't follow), no one has a guarantee that their children will turn from their sin and put their faith in Jesus as their Lord and Savior. Because of that reality, there may come a time when one or more of our children choose a different way (at least for a season) and run from the greatest gift—the one that we have prayed for, pointed them toward, and raised them to take hold of. Like the prodigal son in Luke 15 v 11-32, who rejected his father's wisdom and ran off to foolishly squander his inheritance, our children may reject or resist the wisdom and truth we have pointed them toward and go down a painful and sometimes destructive path, leaving us in a place of anguish and grief.

I once was that "prodigal" child—lost, angry, and struggling to find my identity. I was hardened on the outside but deeply hurting within. The pain of my choices was not only destroying me but creating heartache within our family and leading me to sever my relationships with the people who loved me most.

By God's grace, my parents did not give up on me, despite how tempting that must have been at times. Instead, they entrusted my life to God, loved me despite the way I was treating them, and fought a spiritual battle that I could not (or did not want to) by praying for me—prayers that God eventually graciously answered.

Friend, if you have a hard-hearted, rebellious son or daughter, I challenge you to take up your arms, fight the spiritual battle that rages over them with all of your God-given strength, and refuse to give up on their life. I encourage you to pray these three prayers over children who are wandering.

1. PRAY FOR A HEART OF BROKENNESS, WHATEVER THE EARTHLY COST

It's incredibly hard to pray for anything but a comfortable, successful, and pain-free life for our children. But the greatest eternal good that we can pray for them is their salvation, over their earthly happiness or comfort. We have to fight for them in a world filled with temporary pleasures, self-gratification, and blurry lines—entrusting their lives to our Lord and asking him to bring them home, even if the path of salvation must come through their pain. It took the prodigal son the loss of his wealth, his friends, and his dignity—it took him until he was so hungry that he was longing to eat pig food—to come to himself and resolve to "arise and go to my father" (Luke 15 v 15-18). The road home had to go through the pigs' fields.

I am eternally grateful that my parents loved me enough to pray for me to experience brokenness: a brokenness that would lead to healing—even though my path of brokenness nearly killed me.

After the devastating loss of my identity as an athlete and abuse from peers, my life spiraled out of control. I searched for identity and purpose in anything but Jesus. As self-destructive patterns drove me deeper into despair, I longed for an escape from this world, a desire which ultimately landed me in the protection of a hospital.

In that stark white hospital room, the choice before me was clear: be crushed by the weight of my sin or lay the broken pieces of my life at Christ's feet. I knew what the Bible said about Jesus, and how he always welcomed sinners back into his fold, because my parents had told me that so often. In his grace, God led me to my knees and into his family, and he has been redeeming those broken pieces ever since.

We will only be bold enough to pray a prayer for brokenness over our children when we ourselves have been broken before God and trust his love for our children and for us. It's only when we have completely surrendered our children to him that we can pray, "Father, use what you must to save my child from an eternity apart from you, whatever the cost."

2. PRAY AGAINST THE ENEMY

A battle is being waged over our children's lives. We have to fight for them, especially when blindness keeps them from fighting the battle themselves.

I remember my mom telling me the story of a time when I was standing in the kitchen with her, angry at the world and taking it out on her. She looked at me and said boldly, "I am fighting for you, and I won't let Satan have victory over your life!" After she spoke those words, I fell into a heap on the floor and burst into tears.

We don't have a guarantee of our children's salvation or the outcome we may desire. But we can be confident that God hears our prayers, acts according to his character, and does what is good (though that may be different than what we are asking for). One of the great weapons God has given parents to fight against the world's pull and the enemy's schemes over their children is to pray the way Christ did for Peter:

> *Simon, Simon, behold, Satan demanded to have you, that he might sift you like wheat, but I have prayed for you that your faith may not fail. And when you have turned again, strengthen your brothers.*
> *(Luke 22 v 31-32)*

Peter was a believer, but at the point when he repeatedly denied even knowing Jesus that would have been hard to tell. We cannot know whether or not our wandering children will turn to Christ—but we can still pray to God that he would rescue our children from the power of Satan, give them faith in Christ, and use their lives to advance the gospel and strengthen other believers. And perhaps we can take heart from the knowledge that many of those, like Peter, who have served the Lord the greatest have also known their own days of wandering.

3. PRAY SCRIPTURE OVER THEIR LIFE

Even if your child wants nothing to do with the truth and hates to hear the word of God, they can do nothing to stop you from praying Scripture for them. This is another mighty weapon God has given to parents.

My parents prayed Psalm 18 v 16-19 over my life, and they prayed it often:

> *He sent from on high, he took me;*
> *he drew me out of many waters.*
> *He rescued me from my strong enemy*
> *and from those who hated me,*
> *for they were too mighty for me.*
> *They confronted me in the day of my calamity,*
> *but the Lord was my support.*
> *He brought me out into a broad place;*
> *he rescued me, because he delighted in me.*

It truly amazes me to look back and see how faithful God was in answering this prayer. I was drowning in self-destruction, abuse from others, rebelliousness, and sorrows too deep to understand at the time. God, in his mercy, drew me out of many deep waters and rescued me from my own sin and Satan's desire for me.

As I sat in that hospital room, no longer wanting to live, God rescued me, he brought me out into a broad place, and he showed me that he delighted in me (despite my unworthiness). He has continued to be faithful to this Scripture, upholding me through many deep waters and carrying me through many dark days.

Parents, no matter how far your child seems to be from Jesus or what path they are on, you can fight for their life with the powerful weapon of God's word.

KEEP LOVING THEM

No matter where our children are spiritually or how hard they push us and God's word away, we need to remember to communicate that we are for them, even when we're against their decisions. Despite my parents' disapproval and heartache over the decisions I was making, I somehow knew that, like the prodigal son's father, they were always ready to embrace me with open arms. Rather than communicating that my decisions made me unlovable, they made it clear that my decisions grieved them because I was so deeply loved. They did not pretend that my journey to my own pigs' fields did not matter. But they always made sure that I knew they were ready to embrace me, and that there was a heavenly Father who was ready to do so too. In the end, they didn't save me—but they pointed me to the grace, forgiveness, and unconditional love of my Savior.

No matter what, keep hoping for your children and keep loving them. While there is breath, there is always hope.

THE POWER OF A PRAYING PARENT

The truth is that, while for as long as they are in our home we must teach and train our children, and put boundaries in place, we have no control over their hearts. Ultimately, God alone can fill their hearts with a love for Christ and open their eyes to see the beauty and glory of who he is. It's important to remember that we are here to please Christ, not to save our kids. We can't save them; it was never our job to. But we have a Savior who is able to.

I am learning this on a new level and from a different perspective as I now face struggles with my own children that often tempt me to despair. But we are not helpless, and we are never hopeless. Whether our children are younger or older, and whether they have soft hearts or hearts of stone, we have the power of prayer, God's living word, and a sovereign God who we can trust.

Our Father in heaven loves to take seemingly hopeless lives, as my own once was, and show himself to be merciful and mighty. Give your child the gift of prayer, and trust that God will use his or her life for his good purposes—growing and transforming your own life in the process.

REFLECT

- Are there ways in which deep down you think that your child's salvation depends on you—and so you act accordingly? How does that reveal itself in fear or pride? How would trusting that God is ultimately in control of their salvation, regardless of your success or failure as a parent, change the way you parent and pray?
- Do you believe it's worth praying for your child to experience brokenness if it will lead them to Christ? If not, what is holding you back?
- What verse could you commit to praying for each of your children?
- (Together, if possible) If you have a prodigal child, think about how you can hold firmly to the truth and not ignore or dismiss their sinful choices, yet continually assure them that you are for them and will love them unconditionally. If your children are all following the Lord, praise and thank God for his

gracious kindness and undeserved goodness to you and your children!

PRAY

Lord, the thought of my child rejecting you feels like more than I can bear. But I also feel my inability to change their heart and open their eyes to see their need for you. Often, I carry the guilt and fear that they may turn away from you because of my own sin and failures. Help me to rest and trust in your grace: to know that you alone are able to give them a heart of faith, and that my best efforts won't save them and my worst failures won't place them beyond your reach. Give me the wisdom to love and guide my children and raise them in the truth. In your love and mercy, spare my child from a life of wandering and rebellion, and grant them saving faith in you. And if they wander, do what you must to break the power of sin so that they will surrender their lives to you. Amen.

For further meditation: 1 Samuel 16 v 7; Psalm 139; Jeremiah 24 v 7; Luke 15 v 11-32; 2 Peter 3 v 9.

Journaling

CHAPTER 21

Rediscovering (or Keeping) the Joy

S arah and I sat across the table from each other in
awkward silence. As if we had just ridden that horren-
dous spinning teacup ride at a carnival, we sat there with our
heads still whirling, trying to adjust to our world suddenly
standing still. We had been married 14 years; we still liked
each other (usually), and we were so glad to be out of the
house. So why couldn't we get a simple conversation going?

The problem was this: we had forgotten how to do
anything but survive. We had learned to function well in
chaos, since chaos was all we had known for most of our
marriage. But as time went on, we struggled not to lose
sight of each other.

This is often the natural course for a marriage that has
become defined by suffering. We may still love each other,
and even work well together, but if our relationship mostly
revolves around our trials or the busyness of life and we are
unaware of the danger, our marriage will eventually begin
to suffer. Closeness will be replaced by distance without
us even really noticing, until the gap becomes obvious and
begins to look unbridgeable.

For that reason, I want to encourage you, as we've been
encouraged by others, by sharing some practical ways to

protect your marriage from becoming consumed by your trials. This chapter will look a bit different than the rest of the book in that I'm not going to look to Job for wisdom here; but it's my hope that these suggestions will break any unhelpful patterns of relating to each other solely in the realm of your trials. Of course, this will look different for everyone; it depends on your specific circumstances, but hopefully it will prompt you to look for ways to proactively stay connected with each other on levels other than your struggles.

SPENDING TIME TOGETHER NEEDS PLANNING

It's often much easier to keep our heads down and just keep going. Sometimes the thought of putting effort into asking others for help or hiring a babysitter only adds to our stress. But if we never step out of our chaos, we will get lost in it, and so will our marriage. Sarah and I have learned the importance and necessity of accepting help or hiring babysitters on a consistent basis to change our environment and grow in our knowledge of each other in ways unrelated to our trials. This will look different for each couple, depending on your unique challenges—especially if you are dealing with painful situations within your marriage. But it's important to make an effort to move in the right direction, even if only in small and gradual ways. It may simply be that you decide, "We are going to spend this time together and agree that we will not bring up and will try not to think about what has happened and what is hard right now. Not because it doesn't matter, but because we need to remember what is good about our marriage, rather than what has gone wrong." Here are few things that helped us do that.

1. Stepping outside of your daily routines and trials may at first leave you feeling like a deer in headlights, and that's ok. Many of our dates have begun with us staring blankly at each other, unsure of what to say. We've realized that it's ok to give ourselves the time to process all that's been happening in life, even if it means sitting in silence for a few minutes as we catch our breath and decompress.

2. Buy or print out conversation starters or find a show or podcast that might provoke enjoyable discussion. This has been incredibly helpful for us whenever we get away. Since we're often overwhelmed with life, we can struggle to come up with basic things to talk about that don't revolve around our trials. Asking each other light-hearted questions from a list or engaging in topics unrelated to our daily life often helps us to get to know each other in new ways, to discuss topics to which we never would have given the time of day otherwise, and to connect in areas that have nothing to do with our circumstances.

3. Allot a certain amount of time when you aren't allowed to talk about your trials, your children, or anything else that is currently consuming a lot of your thoughts and time. Of course it's good to connect with each other in those areas as well, but if that is what primarily dominates your relationship, make that topic off limits for a time.

4. Plan a date around an activity. Some of our most refreshing times away together have been dates where we've gone to a one-time painting or cooking class, or we've done something active, like tennis or golf (before Sarah's ankle prevented it). This took the pressure off needing to talk the whole time and gave us something fun to do alongside of each other. When

life is always heavy, it's so important to find new ways to connect and enjoy being around each other that are light-hearted and enjoyable.

5. If you're unable to leave the house, have weekly "in-house dates." Take turns to come up with a new way to spend the time: plan a movie and popcorn, or order take-out and play a favorite game together, or replicate a dinner from your favorite restaurant and set the scene as if you're really there. We can be creative and "shake up" our normal routines without even leaving the house.

GET AWAY FROM "NORMAL"

Spending a few hours as a couple is great—but because it takes a while to decompress when the pressure is really on, if you can manage a couple nights somewhere away from "normal," then it is well worth the cost and the organization. It gives you time to work through the initial "deer in headlights" phase, and still have time to let conversation happen naturally. Changing your surroundings can also be helpful. For example, if a lot of your stress occurs at home, changing your environment (walking through a forest preserve, sitting by a lake, and so on) can help you more quickly connect on a different level.

Maybe even the thought of this brings tears to your eyes because you would give anything to have a reprieve from your current situation but it is simply not an option. If that's the case, remember that God's grace is sufficient for you and your marriage in the circumstances he's allowed. Going away can be helpful, but it isn't a requirement for a good marriage.

FIND A HOBBY TOGETHER

If your marriage is mostly consumed by talking about, enduring, and navigating a trial, it can be helpful and healthy to find something positive to focus on together. Some couples might enjoy taking tennis or golf lessons, cooking classes, gardening together, or refurbishing old furniture. You might even take on the crazy idea of writing a book together! (Full disclosure: doing so does produce its own tensions…) Whatever it is, having something that you and your spouse can work on and accomplish together can help bring balance and health to the marriage as a whole.

ENCOURAGE YOUR SPOUSE TO DO SOMETHING THEY ENJOY

When life is hard, sometimes we feel selfish taking the time or money to do something that isn't absolutely necessary. For example, since Sarah has lost her ability to participate in many of the physical activities that used to be an outlet for her, I have tried to encourage her to find new activities that she would enjoy. I try to offer her a couple of hours when she can go out and write or do something she would find refreshing. Likewise, Sarah encourages me to go out for a run regularly, which is a stress-reducer for me. Whatever our thing may be, we need to encourage each other to see that something that helps rejuvenate us during a stressful season can be a very worthwhile investment. Your spouse may need your "permission" to spend some time doing something they like before they are able to relax and enjoy it.

STAY CONNECTED TO OTHERS

While it's important that we communicate as a couple, it's also healthy for each person to stay connected to other supportive and godly friendships. When we encourage each other to make consistent efforts to spend time with friends, it takes some pressure off of the other spouse and means we can each keep hearing wise counsel and have people to pray with. Good friendships guard a marriage from becoming an echo chamber.

SERVE OTHERS TOGETHER

When your marriage is in a season of trial, it's very easy to become consumed by the difficulties. Unless circumstances prevent it, it can be healthy and helpful to serve others together, especially in your local church. First, it helps to take our eyes off our own suffering and puts our focus on others. Second, it gives us something positive to focus on as a couple and helps keep us connected to the body of Christ, guarding us against isolation.

KEEP (OR START) LAUGHING

It's true that laughter is good medicine. There are countless physical and mental benefits from laughing. In fact, I would even say that one of the greatest gifts to our marriage has been the ability to laugh at the chaos and dysfunction we've lived in. Though some people may raise a brow if they knew what we've learned to laugh about, the truth is that it's helped us cope and keep perspective in our trials. Laughter has diffused tensions, relieved stressful moments, and helped push back the cloud of despair that often threatens to engulf our marriage. Inside jokes that just you and your spouse understand can lighten the atmosphere of your home and marriage, and strengthen your friendship as you bond over laughter, not just tears.

Of course, you may be reading this with a sad heart because you and your spouse have not laughed together in years—and if you're honest, you don't see much to laugh about. You aren't alone in that struggle. When life gets hard or tension builds in our marriage, laughter is often the first thing to go. In seasons like this, we've found it helpful to watch or listen to a comedy movie or (clean) comedian that gives us something to laugh about together. Sometimes, we've needed to focus on something lighthearted outside of our situation to remind ourselves of how to laugh. Does it solve any of our problematic circumstances? No. But it can be refreshing and restorative to have something to smile and laugh about together, even if for a brief time.

Friends, we know full well how quickly marriage can become overwhelmed by the demands, stresses, and trials of life. If we aren't deliberate and proactive, these storms can define and wear down our marriage rather than refine and strengthen it. Though our ultimate hope is not based on anything we do or don't do, there is wisdom in recognizing the pitfalls of being consumed by our suffering, while looking for practical ways to guard against that.

Whether or not you're currently facing a season of hardship in your marriage, remember to invest in and value your friendship with one another. Seasons will come and go, trials will ebb and flow, but the one standing beside you has been given to you to walk with you through it all. Support each other, invest in each other, and remember to enjoy each other.

REFLECT
- As you look back, can you see how trials or the busyness of life have caused your marriage to take the back seat? What are some things you used to enjoy doing together but no longer take the time to do?
- Which of the suggestions in this chapter do you find most helpful, or most challenging?
- What are one or two things that you would enjoy doing with your spouse? What would be enjoyable, refreshing, relaxing, and connecting for you?

- (Together, if possible) Discuss how you feel your marriage is doing in these "practical areas." Decide on one practical step you are going to take in the next couple weeks.

PRAY

Father, when the trials are long and hard, it's hard to think of anything or anyone else. I don't want my marriage to be overwhelmed by suffering, but it threatens to suck the joy, peace, and energy out of our relationship. Help us, Lord. Help us to guard our marriage from being defined by our suffering. Show me how I can support and encourage my husband/ wife and invest in strengthening our relationship. Please provide the wisdom and the means to keep balance and health in our marriage when stress and heartache threaten to consume us. Thank you that you promise to provide all that we need when we look to you as the source of all we need. Amen.

Journaling

CHAPTER 22

God's Answers
to Our "Whys"

*Then the LORD answered Job out of the whirlwind
and said: "Who is this that darkens counsel by
words without knowledge? Dress for action like a
man; I will question you, and you make it known
to me. Where were you when I laid the foundation
of the earth?" (Job 38 v 1-4)*

When trials come, our natural response is to ask
"Why?" We desperately try to create a framework for
them, searching for some semblance of comfort in a purpose
and explanation for our pain.

But often, we can't find any.

For the Christian, we're then immediately faced with a
struggle—the same struggle that Job faced: "If God loves
me, if God is in control, and if God is good... why would
he allow circumstances that seem unloving, out of control,
and far from good? And if he has a purpose for them, why
won't he comfort me with an answer to my questions?"

This road of questioning and confusion is an all-too-
familiar one for me. For most of my life, I've grown up
believing that God is good, sovereign, faithful, and loving.
But I built my belief system in a world that made sense to
me—in circumstances that made those truths easy to accept.

Then life began to unravel. My hopes and expectations were replaced with painful, disappointing, and devastating realities. Like Job, I painfully watched one area of life unravel after another. Marriage, children, motherhood, health, abilities, job, financial comforts, our home… it felt as if nothing was left untouched. So I began to wrestle, for the first time, with the "whys." Why would God, who I've tried to serve and obey, allow all of this? Why does he seem to be against me? Why does he seem silent? Why, when I feel like I'm at my lowest point, would he allow another painful blow? The questions came, but the answers did not.

Though God has been faithful in so many ways, I have been increasingly perplexed and unsettled by his ways. It's hard to trust in the face of unanswered prayers, prayers that are answered with more pain, and times of God's silence when I've longed to hear his voice.

Maybe you've found yourself in a similar place: shaken, confused, and struggling to make sense of the character of God in light of painful circumstances and unanswered prayers.

If so, you're in good company. We, like many who have gone before us, have permission to bring our questions to the Lord in our pain and confusion:

> *Why, O LORD, do you stand far away?*
> *Why do you hide yourself in times of trouble?*
> *(Psalm 10 v 1)*

> *My God, my God, why have you forsaken me?*
> *Why are you so far from saving me … ?*
> *(Psalm 22 v 1)*

> *Why then have you broken down [Jerusalem's] walls … ? (Psalm 80 v 12)*

> *Why have you forgotten me? (Psalm 42 v 9b)*

The psalmists knew the experience of the God whom they thought they knew suddenly seeming strange to them, and of the confidence which they had once put in his promises beginning to waver as their circumstances and feelings argued with what they'd previously held to be true.

This is an unsettling place to be, and it exposes the boundaries we have set on how we think a good and loving God should act, and how far we are willing to trust him. A God we understand is one we're willing to trust, but one whose ways are contrary to ours is disorienting and fear-inducing.

But how do we trust a God we can't understand? God shows us how: we need to look at his answer to Job, and his answer to us in Christ.

SOME UNEXPECTED ANSWERS

Job has a lot of questions for God—and God answers them, but not in the way Job expects. God teaches Job that he won't necessarily get the kind of answer he thinks he wants: namely, the reasons for his sufferings or how long they will last. Through Job, he teaches us the same thing.

Wouldn't you expect God's answer to Job's questions about the fairness of what he's going through to be an explanation of the Lord's exchange with Satan (Job 1)? You'd think God would assure Job that he loved him and never would have brought this upon him if it weren't for the spiritual battle at play. If I were God, I would have justified myself and explained why I was allowing all of Job's suffering, just as I would if one of my kids accused me of intentionally harming them when I was only doing what was best for them and the family in the long run. And certainly, we would assume that God would encourage Job with the fact that his suffering was going to end, and that God was going to restore and bless him in the end!

But God does none of that…

> *Then the* LORD *answered Job out of the whirlwind*
> *and said:*
> *"Who is this that darkens counsel by words*
> *without knowledge?*
> *Dress for action like a man;*
> *I will question you, and you make it known to me.*
>
> *"Where were you when I laid the foundation*
> *of the earth?*
> *Tell me, if you have understanding.*
> *Who determined its measurements—surely you know!*
> *Or who stretched the line upon it?*
> *On what were its bases sunk,*
> *or who laid its cornerstone,*
> *when the morning stars sang together*
> *and all the sons of God shouted for joy?*
>
> *"Or who shut in the sea with doors*
> *when it burst out from the womb,*
> *when I made clouds its garment*
> *and thick darkness its swaddling band,*
> *and prescribed limits for it*
> *and set bars and doors,*
> *and said, 'Thus far shall you come, and no farther,*
> *and here shall your proud waves be stayed'?*
>
> *"Have you commanded the morning since your days*
> *began,*
> *and caused the dawn to know its place … ?"*
>
> *(Job 38 v 1-12)*

Instead of defending himself and explaining himself, God simply reminds Job that he is still in charge and that he knows what he's doing. That's it.

Why? Because the reality is that if God explains this trial to Job, then when Job faces another trial, he'll need that one explained too, and the next one, and the next... and so his faith will actually be shriveling rather than growing. Whereas if God simply reminds Job of who he is and what he can do, then Job will be pushed, painfully but graciously, to trust God.

So God reminds Job of his power, majesty, and wisdom. If he has laid the foundations of the earth, surely he could have prevented Job's calamity. If he sees, cares, and provides when mountain goats give birth, the hawk spreads its wings, and the eagles mount up (39 v 1-4, 26-27), surely he sees, cares, and will provide for us. We don't need to know the answers so much as we need to know *him*.

Friends, our questions and doubts won't be answered by making sense of our circumstances and shrinking our view of God so that we understand him. And our questions being answered won't actually help us to trust Christ more—they will only cause us to trust him when there's a reason that makes sense to us. No, our questions and doubts will only be satisfied when we begin to grasp the majesty, power, and sovereignty of our Creator, Savior and Lord, and when we believe that he remains in control and knows what he is doing. We will only come to trust him with a deeply humble and quiet posture when we begin to grasp even a fragment of his true glory and can say with the psalmist:

> *What is man that you are mindful of him,*
> *and the son of man that you care for him?*
> *(Psalm 8 v 4)*

Job's "whys" were answered when God reminded him of his own character, and ours can be too. Not only because we are the clay in the hands of the Potter (Isaiah 29 v 16) but because we can trust that if God set the foundation of the earth and marked its dimensions, he has set boundaries to our suffering for his sovereign and holy purposes.

JESUS ASKED "WHY?"

And about the ninth hour Jesus cried out with a loud voice, saying ... "My God, my God, why have you forsaken me?" (Matthew 27 v 46)

Jesus knew the plan of salvation, and knew why he was hanging on his cross—and that resurrection lay ahead. Yet still he cried out to his Father "Why?" as he endured the pain of the cross. God didn't answer his cries with an answer in that moment—rather, he answered them by taking what seemed hopeless and pointless and bringing salvation hope to the world through it.

At the cross it looked as if death had won, as if God was not in control, and as if God didn't love his Son. But in truth, the cross was the greatest picture of God's sovereignty, love, and goodness, far beyond what our minds ever could have comprehended had we been there at that moment. We have the blessing, living after the resurrection of Christ from the dead, of seeing why he hung there, and seeing that God was still in charge and truly knew what he was doing. Praise God that he doesn't act according to what makes sense to us but what truly is best for us!

WHAT WE DO KNOW IS BETTER THAN WHAT WE DON'T

So, when we are faced with trials that just don't make sense to us, we can draw near to God and ask "Why?," but most of all we need to turn our eyes to the cross—the ultimate assurance that our God is wholly good, in control, and trustworthy. If he loved us enough to sacrifice his own Son for us, we can trust that same sovereign love when our "whys" seem to go unanswered.

In the end, Job reminds us that God does not owe us an explanation. Rather than trying to make up an explanation ourselves (when, like Job, we most likely couldn't even imagine the true explanation!), we remember that the Lord is good, purposeful, and loving in all he does, even when we cannot understand his ways or feel his presence in the darkness. We need to know the character of God more than we need to understand the course of our lives.

Whether your marriage seems to be in shambles, or your hearts are grieving over the illness or death of a loved one, or your once-comfortable life is now a distant memory, you can bring your confusion and dismay and fall to your knees in humble surrender to your Savior. His ways are far greater than you can comprehend, and his silence is not evidence of his absence. He desires for you to trust and fear him by faith, with an unshakable hope in his unchanging character. As C.H. Spurgeon said:

> *"God delivers His servants in ways that exercise their faith. He would not have them lacking in faith, for faith is the wealth of the heavenly life. He desires that the trial of faith continues until faith grows strong and comes to full assurance. The sycamore fig never ripens into sweetness unless it is bruised; the same is true of faith. Tested believer, God will bring you through, but do not expect Him to bring you through in the way that human reason suggests, for that would not develop your faith."*
>
> *(Beside Still Waters, page 148)*

We need to encourage ourselves with these truths, and we need to encourage and pray for our spouse as well—to pray first and foremost that they'd know more of God, rather than that they'd understand what's going on or even that they'd get beyond their trial.

The joy and peace you desire, and that your spouse desires, are not found in understanding your circumstances, or in having a better relationship with your spouse, or in your prayers being answered as you desire, as wonderful as those things are. No, the true joy you seek is found in Christ himself and is often experienced most deeply when you believe that he is enough and is worthy of being trusted when you can't make sense of his ways.

We never see Job learn the "why" behind his suffering. But he came to believe, at a far deeper level, who God was and why he was worthy to be trusted. May that be true for each one of us as we navigate the trials of this life. We may grieve, wrestle, and lament, but as we do, may we all come to know that God is still in charge, and that he knows what he is doing.

REFLECT

- Has there been a time in your life when, like Job, you questioned why God has allowed something painful? If so, did you bring your struggles and questions to Christ or did your questions lead you toward anger and bitterness toward God?
- What do you make of the way in which God answered Job's questions? If you put your own questions and circumstances in place of Job's, how would God's answer in Job 38 – 41 give you comfort and peace? If they don't, why do you think that is?
- (Together, if possible) Share with each other your "why" questions. Then share with each other what God's answer to Job has taught you and how it could give new perspective to your current circumstances. If

you are both willing to, spend time praying together, being honest with the Lord about your struggles and questions, but then thanking and praising him for who he is and that you can trust him.

PRAY

Jesus, I often wonder "why": why have you allowed this storm in my life; why didn't you prevent it when I know that you could have; and why haven't you answered my prayers in the way I had hoped? I believe you are good, but at times I struggle to understand your purposes and ways. But maybe I'm not meant to understand all of your ways, and need to learn to trust you instead. Forgive me for when I've questioned your character, grown angry and bitter, or tried to make you into a God who makes sense to me. You are my Creator, Sustainer, Healer, and Savior. You don't owe me answers. When I struggle to understand, help me to trust who you are and rest in the love that you have showed in the greatest way possible: on the cross—giving your own life for my forgiveness, freedom, and joy. Help me to rest in that love when I want answers; help me to trust in your power and goodness when I want control; and lead me to worship and praise you all the more as I wait for your plan to unfold in my heart and life. Amen.

For further meditation: Psalm 13; Habakkuk 1 v 1 – 2 v 4; 3 v 17-19; Isaiah 40 v 28-31; Isaiah 55 v 8-9.

Journaling

CHAPTER 23

From Hearing to Seeing: The Fruit of Humility

I know that you can do all things, and that no purpose of yours can be thwarted. I had heard of you by the hearing of the ear, but now my eye sees you; therefore I despise myself, and repent in dust and ashes. (Job 42 v 2, 5-6)

I f it wasn't for the Lord taking our marriage through many painful trials, I would be a far prouder man and a less loving husband and father.

That is because God has used difficult, unchosen circumstances to humble me—to see that reliance on him and trusting him in discomfort leads to greater freedom and joy. Though I naturally want to be right in my marriage, God has shown me that there's greater blessing in creating an environment of openness, trust, and intimacy than in winning the argument. Though I want to appear strong and wise, and have well-behaved children and a struggle-free marriage, God has humbled me to see that those things would keep me satisfied in my independence when, in reality, I am a far stronger, wiser man when I realize how dependent I am on Christ. Humility is a blessing—and so, while the path to it may be painful, it is one that is worthwhile to walk along.

WHAT IS HUMILITY?

We meet Job in chapter 42 despising himself and repenting in dust and ashes. Though Job at first mourned in ashes and now repents in ashes (compare 2 v 8 and 42 v 6), something has changed along the way. He has gone from hearing to seeing God. The turning point in his suffering, and the good that God was bringing through it all, was when he could finally say, "I had heard of you by the hearing of the ear, but now my eye sees you" (42 v 5).

Part of what he "sees" is that he had far too high a view of himself and far too low a view of God—and now he has a right view of both himself and God, so he lowers himself and repents of his pride. Humility both shows us that we need to repent (because we've been proud and had too high a view of ourselves, our plans, our goodness, and so on) and enables us to repent (because now we're not too proud, so we stop making excuses, justifying ourselves, blaming our circumstances or our spouse, and so on). As with Job, what God is doing through all of our suffering is to grow us from hearing about him to seeing and more deeply knowing him. C.H. Spurgeon wrote, "In prosperity, God is heard, and that is a blessing. In adversity, God is seen, and that is a greater blessing." This is the path to humility.

We are naturally bent toward pride—to seeing ourselves as the center of our marriage, family, work, and, quite honestly, the universe. Humility involves accepting that we aren't the center of the universe: God is, and we revolve around him. So when we think of ourselves less and of him more, we have a right view of ourselves and of others, and of our place regarding others and him. "Humility is not thinking less of yourself, but thinking of yourself less," as C.S. Lewis is reputed to have said. This means, as it did for Job, seeing yourself rightly: you don't know everything, you don't have all the answers, your plans for your life aren't necessarily best, and, put bluntly, you don't deserve better. And it means seeing God rightly: he does know everything, he does have all the answers, his plans are best, and he deserves your praise and obedience.

Seeing ourselves as we really are, and God as he really is, will always lead to repentance, especially for our pride in thinking that we are better and bigger than we really are, and that we're at the center of everything (which is what Job struggled with in questioning God). The problem wasn't that Job brought his questions to God—it was his assumption that God owed him an explanation. It's not that it's wrong to ask questions of God and lament our suffering, nor even to ask him to show us a glimpse of how he is at work for good; but it is wrong to question God with a sense of "I know better than you, so you should do things my way."

So how do we reach the kind of humility that Job arrived at?

HOW WE ARE HUMBLED

How did Job's humility grow as he went from hearing of God to seeing and knowing God?

Job's suffering took what he believed to be true of God in theory, put it to the test, and brought him through that test now knowing his belief to be true as a lived reality. The same process is often needed in our lives. We may say we believe something, but we don't really see and know what we believe until it's been put to the test.

Imagine a place that you've heard about—it may be a mighty waterfall, a canyon, a historic landmark, or a mountaintop view. You've been told about its breathtaking beauty, magnificent structure, or awesome power. You can try to imagine how amazing it must be, but you're limited in your understanding, having only heard of its existence.

Then you visit it yourself. Now you experience it first-hand—the size of it makes you feel small and insignificant, the history makes you realize how quickly life comes and goes, or the power makes you feel powerless and aware of how little control you have.

This is a little like our journey from believing what we hear about God to seeing his presence, power, and holiness first-hand. Trials are often the lenses through which we are able to see him like this. That was certainly the case for Job.

Job had believed he loved God above all, but now he knew his God was greater than his losses. In chapter 1 verse 1, if we'd asked Job, "Do you live in awe of God, and do you love God more than the things he gives?" he'd no doubt have said "Yes." And he'd have been right. But if we asked him the same question in chapter 42, he'd have said "Yes" with a far greater appreciation of what he was saying, and he'd have meant it far more, because now he'd lost those things God gave, and he'd seen that God was still there, still sovereign, still somehow good. He had already believed God to be faithful, but he now had seen God's faithfulness through and in the worst of his own circumstances. He had believed he was an unworthy sinner in theory, but now he could see his sin and unworthiness before a holy God. He had believed God to be sovereign, but now he knew God to be sovereign even when he couldn't understand God. He had believed God to be good when all was well, but now he had seen the depths of God's goodness in light of the redemption that would one day come, which no storm could sweep away (Job 19 v 25-27).

Though it's often so hard to see in the moment, the same is true for us. Everything God allows in our lives, including the trials we face in and against our marriage, is meant to open our eyes to who our Creator is and who we are in Christ, so that we might be humbled, grow in righteousness, and reflect more of him. It's not until we're brought low and see how little we really deserve that we begin to grasp the incredible blessings we have in Christ, both now and eternally. As he did in Job's life, God uses our suffering to cultivate the fruit of humility so that in due time he will lift us up, giving us greater freedom and joy even within our hardships. Peter put it this way: "Humble yourselves, therefore, under the mighty hand of God so that at the proper time he may exalt you, casting all your anxieties on him, because he cares for you" (1 Peter 5 v 6-7).

Though the world tells us to elevate ourselves, God commands us to humble ourselves. In God's economy, the way up is the way down; the path to increase is to decrease; and to be strong we must come to him in our weakness. Because God promises to enable what he commands of us, he allows suffering to produce a humility in us that we cannot produce in ourselves in order to exalt us with him in his glory.

The path to humility may be difficult, but it is a path of God's grace. He allows suffering to humble us so that, in time, we will be lifted up to Christ and be made like him.

HOW HUMILITY HELPS YOUR MARRIAGE

Though we don't enjoy being humbled, we will enjoy being humble, and our marriages will enjoy the product of our humility. The more we see God and are humbled, the more we begin to reflect his character. And the more we reflect Christ, the more we will be a blessing to our husband or wife.

I know this personally. Though we have a long way to go, the humbling work that God has done in Sarah and I through our many different trials has been a hard-fought but worthwhile blessing to our marriage. Over time, it has increased our compassion toward each other as we grieve and respond to our trials in different ways. It's grown our patience with each other as we struggle with our own weaknesses and sins. It's led us to pray more consistently, realizing that we don't have the ability to change or help each other, our marriage, or our circumstances without God's help. Growing in humility has led us to communicate more honestly, and listen more openly, understanding that though struggles and hurts will happen, we honor each other and the Lord when we share and seek to empathize with each other, and then face our trials together. And last, but certainly not least, the fruit of humility through our trials has taught us to be quicker to apologize and quicker to forgive, realizing that we are both undeserving of and dependent on Christ's grace and forgiveness.

The road has been difficult, and we still have a long way to go—but by the grace of God, the fruit of humility will continue to transform our marriage and our perspective on the difficulties we face within our marriage.

But for that to happen, I have to keep being willing to be humbled. That means being quicker to look at myself and my weaknesses and the areas in which I need to repent than to see Sarah's mistakes. It means accepting that I haven't arrived. It means looking for what God is up to when a new storm comes our way, and accepting that sometimes I won't be able to see the answer. Trials in and around my marriage won't automatically bring humility—trials can also breed pride, self-pity, and disappointment with or bitterness toward the other. I have to choose that, for my part, I am going to let God reshape me, and not harden myself against him and Sarah.

Brother and sister, I don't assume that I know or understand the challenges or trials you are facing—and I certainly don't have all the answers to them. But I do know that the trials in your life and marriage can drive you to a greater

Humility means being quicker to look at my weaknesses than her mistakes, and it means looking for what God is up to when a new storm comes and accepting that sometimes I won't be able to see the answer.

dependence on Christ. Allow your losses and disappointments to remind you of who you are not, and who God is. Resist the temptation in suffering to put yourself in the center as Job had started to do, as though you—or your spouse— are the most important person in the world, as Job had started to do. Remember that God's plans are greater than ours and he knows what we do not. Then you will be made more humble, reflect Christ more, and be a blessing to your spouse as a result.

Would you join me in praying this?

> *Whatever it takes, Lord, humble us to depend on you, delight in you, desire you, and trust you as Lord.*

Nothing is beyond God's ability to transform and renew. He can heal brokenness, repair and protect marriages, and bring blessing out of suffering. But it begins with bringing ourselves before him in humility and faith, and if that has not been your perspective up to this point, then there is no better day to start walking that road than today.

REFLECT

- After reading this chapter, do you still find it hard to view humility as a blessing? If so, it's good to ask, "Would I rather have comfort now, and not experience the eternal blessings Christ wants to give me, or am I willing to trust the Lord with what is difficult now, knowing that there will be greater blessing in the end?"
- Is there a struggle in your marriage in which pride is at the center? Are you trying to control a situation, and are you unwilling to hear your spouse's point of view? Are you pursuing your own comfort over what is best for your spouse and your marriage?

- How have you seen God use your trials to work humility in your life and your marriage? How does this encourage you?
- (Together, if possible) From the section in this chapter on "How Humility Helps Your Marriage," what are one or two ways in which you can see that God is growing this in your hearts?

PRAY

Jesus, I admit that I too often desire my own glory above yours. I'd rather be strong than feel my weakness; and I'd rather argue that I'm right than humbly admit when I'm wrong. Help me to see that humility is a blessing, and use these trials to produce the fruit of humility in me and my marriage. Whatever it takes, help me to not waste these difficult days but to trust that you are using them in my life so that I will see and know you with a deeper and more dependent faith. Whatever it takes, remind me that my marriage and this life are not about me, and I am not in control. Whatever it takes, humble me and test me so that the overflow of my heart is to worship, praise, and glorify you. Whatever it takes, let me feel my need for you so that I will find my complete satisfaction and joy in you alone. Whatever it takes, may your Spirit lead me in obedience and faithfulness to lay down my wants and desires in my marriage and to consider my husband/wife more significant than myself. Amen.

For further meditation: Deuteronomy 8 v 2-10, 16; Psalm 25 v 9; Philippians 2 v 3-8; James 4 v 6-10; 1 Peter 5 v 5-8.

Journaling

_____

_____

_____

_____

_____

_____

_____

_____

_____

_____

_____

_____

_____

_____

_____

_____

_____

_____

_____

_____

CHAPTER 24

The Glue That Keeps You Together: Forgiveness

*Now therefore take seven bulls and seven rams and
go to my servant Job and sacrifice a burnt offering
for yourselves. My servant Job will pray for you,
and I will accept his prayer and not deal with you
according to your folly. (Job 42 v 8)*

I squirmed in my seat as our pastor spoke on the importance of honesty and forgiveness in our marriages and the thought formed in my mind.

"You've sinned against Jeff, Sarah."

The Holy Spirit's conviction churned in my gut, however hard I tried to reason it away. "There's no point in telling Jeff. It will only hurt him. Besides, it's between me and the Lord," I thought. The next words out of the pastor's mouth seemed directed right at me: "Is there anything between you and your spouse that you need to be honest about? Don't believe the lie that it's better to keep it in the dark." I knew that the Lord was asking me to humble myself and confess my struggle with this particular sin—not only to the Lord, but to Jeff.

Later, through tears, I shared with Jeff this sin that I had committed against him and asked for his forgiveness. Despite fear, a basketful of excuses, and humiliation screaming at me to stop, I admitted that I was wrong and was ready to accept the consequences.

And Jeff forgave me. He was hurt, but he was also compassionate and gentle. We've not always been so quick to confess and repent, or so quick to forgive and restore our relationship—but this time we were, and it made our marriage far stronger than continuing with hidden sins or unresolved hurt. Forgiveness is essential, even when—especially when—it goes against every natural bone in our body. If you've been married for more than 24 hours, I'm sure that you can relate.

When the pressure's on, our natural sinful tendencies rise to the surface. Heat reveals imperfections before it burns them away, and so forgiveness becomes key in our trials. We (as individuals and as a couple) don't suddenly get more sinful when the storm comes. We were already sinful, but the storm exposes it. So a book on marriage needs a chapter on forgiveness. Job 42 v 7-9 is a very interesting part of the conclusion, and thankfully it touches on various aspects of that forgiveness:

> After the LORD had said these things to Job, he said to Eliphaz the Temanite, "I am angry with you and your two friends, because you have not spoken the truth about me, as my servant Job has. So now take seven bulls and seven rams and go to my servant Job and sacrifice a burnt offering for yourselves. My servant Job will pray for you, and I will accept his prayer and not deal with you according to your folly. You have not spoken the truth about me, as my servant Job has." So Eliphaz the Temanite, Bildad the Shuhite and Zophar the Naamathite did what the Lord told them; and the LORD accepted Job's prayer. (NIV)

I find this fascinating (even if a little complex!) and incredibly helpful in understanding the facets of repentance and forgiveness, both with God and with each other. Here are a few ways to apply what God says to Job to our own lives and marriages.

AS GOD IN CHRIST FORGAVE YOU

This passage in Job shows us what it takes to be forgiven by God. You need a sacrifice that will bear God's judgment on your sin—death—in your place. And you need a mediator to speak to God on your behalf, so that God "will accept [their] prayer and not deal with [you] according to [your] folly" (v 8). This forgiveness is what God is extending to Job's proud, presumptuous friends here.

The sacrifice Job's friends were to offer—seven bulls and rams—was very costly, but it was still only animals. And the mediator they were told to come to God through was righteous, but Job was still only an imperfect human. Both are meant to point us forward: to the ultimate sacrifice, where God in Christ bore his own judgment; and to the ultimate mediator, God's Son himself, who offers his self-sacrifice to God and speaks on our behalf.

Have you ever realized what it took God to forgive you? It's only if you stand in awe of God's forgiveness of you, and what it cost him in Christ, that you'll ever be in a position where you are able to forgive—to bear the cost of giving up your own right to anger and hurt so that a relationship can be restored. That's why the New Testament often links God's forgiveness of us to our forgiveness of others: "Be kind to one another, tenderhearted, forgiving one another, as God in Christ forgave you" (Ephesians 4 v 32).

When we're unwilling to forgive, it's because we've forgotten that we are in need of divine forgiveness ourselves.

When we say we can't forgive, we're actually saying we won't bear the cost of it, despite the cost that God bore to forgive us.

THE DIFFERENCE BETWEEN VERTICAL AND HORIZONTAL FORGIVENESS

If we're not careful, however, we could read this passage in Job and oversimplify forgiveness, thinking that if we just choose to forgive (or ask for forgiveness) as God commands, restoration will follow and all will be well.

But more often than not, that's far from what we experience. So we naturally struggle with questions such as: What if our spouse is unrepentant? Do we still have to forgive them?

I have found *Forgiving Others*, a short book by the author and counselor Timothy Lane, incredibly helpful in understanding the difference between vertical forgiveness (between us and God) and horizontal forgiveness (between us and others). He points out two verses that seem to contradict each other but that in fact help us walk wisely as we pursue reconciliation:

> *And when you stand praying, if you hold anything against anyone, forgive him, so that your Father in heaven may forgive you your sins. (Mark 11 v 25, NIV)*

> *Pay attention to yourselves! If your brother sins, rebuke him, and if he repents, forgive him. (Luke 17 v 3)*

Dr. Lane writes:

> *"These two verses seem to contradict each other, so which is true? Both! In these two verses we have two axis of forgiveness: the vertical and the horizontal. In Mark 11 v 25 we see the vertical axis: man to*

God. It deals with my own heart attitude toward the person before God. It calls me to repent of bitterness and forgive. Forgiveness as an attitude (the vertical dimension) must be present in my heart first.

"Luke 17 v 3, on the other hand, speaks to the horizontal axis of forgiveness: person to person. Forgiveness as a transaction between two people is possible only if the offender repents, admits the sin, and asks for forgiveness. But even if the offender does not repent, the offended person must maintain forgiveness as an attitude in the vertical dimension. You cannot use the offender's failure to seek forgiveness as an excuse to hold onto your anger and hurt." (page 15)

I find this distinction so helpful. In the book of Job, God was the one who moved Job's friends to repentance. Job had rightfully confronted them about their hurtful accusations (Job 21 v 27, 34), but he couldn't make them see their sin, and he couldn't force their repentance. But when God confronted their sin, Job's heart had been made ready in a vertical sense to pray on their behalf and restore the relationship with his friends in a horizontal sense.

The same is true for us in marriage. We should be honest with our spouse about how they have hurt or wronged us, but we can't force them to see their sin, repent, and begin the process of reconciliation and healing. But if we rely on the Holy Spirit to empower us to forgive in the vertical sense, we will be ready to forgive and be reconciled when or if they do seek our forgiveness.

There may be times, however, when a spouse may choose to continue in their sin, and understanding vertical and horizontal forgiveness will help us navigate that situation wisely. First, when we understand that we're called to forgive by entrusting our spouse's sin to the Lord, it guards us from the bitterness and anger that will take root if we're unwilling to forgive them before the Lord, who will one day bring all sins to account (except for those forgiven in Christ).

Second, understanding what God's word says and doesn't say about forgiveness will help us navigate our marriage if our spouse continues in an unrepentant and hurtful manner. There may be times when we need to enlist outside help, or even remove ourselves from the situation for a time (under the guidance of our local church, or governing authorities if any kind of abuse has occurred) to allow room for repentance to happen. The command to forgive is not a demand that we remain in a vulnerable and unhealthy situation. It's actually unloving to remain in a situation that enables another's continued sin, and, though we can forgive in the vertical sense, it is wise and loving to take necessary actions to seek outside help and biblical counsel in hopes of eventual restoration. Though God always commands us to forgive in our hearts before him, we can't force repentance and reconciliation from a spouse who is unwilling. When Paul tells us to live at peace with others, he prefaces the command with eleven crucial words: "*If it is possible, as far as it depends on you,* live at peace with everyone" (Romans 12 v 18, NIV, my emphasis).

FORGIVENESS IS AN EVENT AND A PROCESS

I wonder if Job ever struggled again with remembering how his friends, family, and wife added to his misery in his lowest moments. I know that I would have.

So I need to remember that forgiveness is both an event and a process. Here's Timothy Lane again:

> "*When we forgive someone, it is an event: 'I forgive you.' But that is not the end of the matter. Every*

time I remember the offense, I must continue to forgive. 'I forgive you and will continue to forgive you.'" (pages 8-9)

Choosing to forgive doesn't necessarily mean that the hurt, lack of trust, or anger will suddenly disappear. Forgiveness is a process that may take time as we rely on Christ's strength to enable us to continually give up our hurt and anger, fight the temptation to rehearse the wrong, be willing to look at our own sin as well as someone else's, and seek to rebuild trust.

In marriage this is important to remember when you've been hurt, but it's also good to remember when you're the one who's hurt your spouse. Even if they have forgiven you as "an event," you need to be patient with them because healing and rebuilding trust take time. With patience, prayer, and the help of the Holy Spirit, God can redeem and restore the brokenness and damage done from our sin, but it will often take time and an ongoing willingness—in both husband and wife—to rely on Christ's strength and healing power.

A MARRIAGE MARKED BY FORGIVENESS

Unless you and your spouse are perfect (which is unlikely!), to have a happy marriage you are going to need to have both honesty (about how the other has hurt you, but also about how you have sinned against the other) and forgiveness (on both sides). We need to be willing to assume the best about each other and be slow to react to each other's faults—not assuming the worst or ascribing suspect motives to each other's actions, but, at times, making allowance for our spouse's weaknesses for the sake of unity (Ephesians 4 v 2-3).

Here are some questions for you to consider on your own, and then, if you're able to, to discuss with your spouse:

1. *Is there something I'm annoyed or bitter about, that actually doesn't need forgiveness?* A lot of what leads to tension and irritation in a marriage is caused by the reality that a husband and wife are two different people, who respond differently to and communicate differently about joys and sorrows. Have you been viewing your spouse's differences as sin? Or have you been nursing a grievance that is larger than any sin that might have been committed?

2. *Is there anything I need to ask forgiveness for, instead of holding onto my justifications or pride?* (And ask your spouse: Are there areas of hurt that you have not told me about because you're worried about my excuses, anger, retaliation, or denial?)

3. *Is there anything I need to grant forgiveness for, instead of holding onto my hurt and anger?*

4. *Is there anything I need to accept forgiveness for, instead of punishing myself about something for which Christ died?*

Friends, learning to give and receive forgiveness is one of the greatest ways you can live out the gospel within your marriage. Grow in gratitude for what Christ has done for you and be motivated to unconditionally love and forgive the one beside you—for a marriage that exudes grace-filled forgiveness is a marriage that will experience God's riches of peace, unity and life.

REFLECT

- Has this chapter changed your view of forgiveness in any way?
- Is there an area where you have extended forgiveness or received forgiveness but continue to struggle with hurt, trust, or shame? How can understanding forgiveness as both an event and a process help you move forward?

- (Together, if possible) Work through the four questions on the previous page. (You might find it most fruitful to work through them on your own and then share your answers, listening to each other's insights).

PRAY

Jesus, thank you for loving me to the point of sacrificing your own life in order that I might be forgiven and given a new heart and life in you. Though that should make me quick to forgive and ask for forgiveness from my spouse and others, I admit that I still struggle to at times. Help me to grasp how much grace and forgiveness I have received at such cost to you, and grow me in extending and receiving that grace and forgiveness to and from others in both the vertical sense and the horizontal sense (when it's possible). I want my marriage to be filled with forbearance, repentance, forgiveness, and reconciliation when it's needed, and I need your help with that—we both do. Give us your grace to enable us to grow in this area, to experience the blessings of it, and to be a reflection of your gospel. Amen.

For further meditation: Psalm 103 v 10-14; Proverbs 28 v 13; Micah 7 v 18-19; Matthew 18 v 20-35; 1 John 1 v 9.

Journaling

CHAPTER 25

The Best Is Yet to Come

And the LORD restored the fortunes of Job … And the LORD blessed the latter days of Job more than his beginning. (Job 42 v 10, 12)

In the last seven verses of the book of Job "the LORD restored the fortunes of Job … and gave him twice as much as before" (v 10). It's a happy ending—he finishes more blessed than he started, with twice as many animals, another ten children, and many more years of a full life (v12-13, 16-17). Job gets his happy ending—and that's hard, if you feel that there's no happy ending for you in sight. "Ok, but what about me?" we ask. "Will my marriage be restored? Will my body ever be healed? Will my losses ever be redeemed? How do I not lose hope?" You might be tempted to feel discouraged.

Brother, sister, we're right there with you. We'd love to be able to end this book by saying that we've experienced restoration in our many trials as Job did at last. But we haven't. Our bodies are still sick, our children are still suffering, our finances are draining, our marriage still needs work and, as of this week, our house is infested with fleas. That is not our idea of restoration and redemption.

And yet, at the same time, we are not without hope and joy. God has done, and is doing, a mighty work of redemption and restoration. He is changing our hearts, growing our marriage, increasing our love for his Son, and filling us with anticipation of the eternal restoration that is coming. And the truth is that we—and you—can look forward to something far better than the last seven verses of Job.

A HOPE WORTH WALKING TOWARD

The Christian life is all about future hope. We will end, as Job ends, with restoration. John describes our future hope in Revelation 21 v 1-4:

> *Then I saw a new heaven and a new earth, for the first heaven and the first earth had passed away, and the sea was no more. And I saw the holy city, new Jerusalem, coming down out of heaven from God, prepared as a bride adorned for her husband. And I heard a loud voice from the throne saying, "Behold, the dwelling place of God is with man. He will dwell with them, and they will be his people, and God himself will be with them as their God. He will wipe away every tear from their eyes, and death shall be no more, neither shall there be mourning, nor crying, nor pain anymore, for the former things have passed away."*

One day, pain, tears, grief, disappointments, illnesses, death, striving, and sin will be no more, and every follower of Jesus will be in the presence of Jesus. Our imperfect marriages will be replaced with the perfect marriage of Christ and his people; dysfunctional and broken families will be replaced with perfect unity and love in all God's family; and our broken bodies will be replaced with painless, whole, everlasting bodies. There will be no more need for doctors, medicine, or funerals; no more struggling relationships, broken homes, or lost loved ones; and no more fears, failures, or sin. And none of that is the greatest gift. The highpoint of the new creation will be that we finally dwell in the presence of Christ, face to face, experiencing the fullness of his glory. Our faith will at last be made sight, and we will live in a world that needs no sun because Christ himself will be our light. We will walk with him, talk with him, and enjoy him forever. Jesus will wipe away every tear from our eyes, our sorrow will be no more, and our righteousness will be complete in his presence. Though it's hard to wrap our minds around, it's the hope we must cling to as we walk through the storms to reach our heavenly home.

LIFE IN THE LAND BETWEEN

God can restore our losses now if he chooses to (and we should be prayerful to that end, watchful for it, and thankful if and when we see it)—but some things will not be restored on this earth. It was the same for Job himself. Though God blessed and restored to him twice as much as before in terms of animals, he was given the same number of children as he had previously lost. Why was he not given double the amount of children as well? Perhaps because the ten precious children he had lost were awaiting him in glory.

Though we tend to focus on all that God restored to Job and his wife (which reminds us of his great compassion), we need to remember that some of what they lost was not restored in their lifetime (reminding us that this isn't our home). Though I'm sure they rejoiced and loved their subsequent ten children, Job and his wife couldn't replace (or restore) the children they had lost. Instead, they enjoyed what God had restored in their earthly life, while presumably still longing for the day when they would be reunited with their children in complete restoration.

Christian, we have to remember this, in both life and marriage. Until we reach our heavenly home, we live in the land between—as God's redeemed people in a fallen world, on the way to a perfect one. That means grieving the losses that may not be restored in our lifetime. It means praying for and pursuing growth and restoration where possible. But above all, it means that we hold all things loosely, trusting that Christ is at work in ways that we often can't see, working to restore us to himself, cultivating greater joy and satisfaction in him, and preparing us for our heavenly home—and strengthening our marriages through the storms.

So, don't give up hope for now. Things can change; God can work; tomorrow may be better than today. But don't stake all your hope on now, either. Wait and pray with the expectation that he can restore, heal, and redeem your circumstances and marriage in his perfect timing, but do so knowing that he will, one day, fully restore and redeem everything to perfection in his presence. It is true for every follower of Jesus that "after you have suffered a little while, the God of all grace, who has called you to his eternal glory in Christ, will himself restore, confirm, strengthen, and establish you" (1 Peter 5 v 10).

This is what Job glimpsed and trusted God for. Before Job saw the earthly blessing and restoration of Job 42, he had already discovered that he had what he most needed: the living, redeeming God, who would stand on this earth and live with his people beyond the judgment (19 v 25)— the all-powerful, completely sovereign, totally good God (42 v 2-6). Job was able to look up and look forward even in the depths, and so also in the heights.

We—whatever we are lacking or mourning—have greater reason than Job to do the same. We can look back at the resurrection of Jesus to assure us that the One we are pinning our hopes on is real, is powerful, and keeps his promises. It's the resurrection that Peter pointed his suffering friends to, urging them to look forward and look up:

Blessed be the God and Father of our Lord Jesus Christ! According to his great mercy, he has caused us to be born again to a living hope through the resurrection of Jesus Christ from the dead, to an inheritance that is imperishable, undefiled, and unfading, kept in heaven for you, who by God's power are being guarded through faith for a salvation ready to be revealed in the last time.

(1 Peter 1 v 3-5)

So whatever else you do and whatever else comes your way, place and then keep your faith in this God whom Job knew. It is possible that restoration, perhaps beyond your imagination, will come in your marriage or in your circumstances. But it may not, because this is a fallen and often confusing world. You can't control such restoration, nor demand it. Your part is to cling to Christ, whatever your situation or the state of your marriage, determining, with God's help, to keep looking up and looking forward. That—whether or not your spouse realizes it or appreciates it—is the best thing you can do for your marriage and for your souls.

TOGETHER THROUGH THE STORMS

(Jeff) As Sarah and I continue to navigate our own hard road—one that has tested our faith and our marriage at every turn—we have seen God's faithfulness carry us through, humbling us, changing us, and growing us. It hasn't been easy or what we expected, and it certainly hasn't been on our timetable, but as we take our eyes off ourselves and each other, and fix them on Christ, we can see that he has been doing a work of restoration in our hearts and marriage, deepening our longing for him above all else. As sinners, we still fail each other. We struggle with what we don't understand and long for relief from our earthly trials. But, by

God's grace, the storms we're facing have not destroyed us. Instead, they are driving us ever more deeply into the love, comfort, and strength of Christ, where we are discovering a surprising and ongoing source of restoration and blessing in our marriage, even as we long for our eternal home.

So as we come to the final section of the final chapter, I'd love for you to put the book down and reflect on what you've read and learned along the way. Ask the Holy Spirit to show you some specific changes that you can make within your marriage. Rather than focusing on the storms against and within your marriage, which may seem insurmountable, think of a few things (and they may be fairly small things) that you can and will positively do, change, or commit to. Perfection is not our aim, but pursuing growth and taking practical steps of faith will not only be a blessing to your life, but your marriage as well.

Then write them down, which will help you make them specific and encourage you to commit to them.

If you are able to, discuss them with your spouse, asking them to help you, encourage and challenge you, and pray for you. Ideally, think through ways you are going to pursue change together.

But if that isn't possible, you can still commit to areas that you'd like to grow in with the Lord's help, to please Christ as you serve and love your spouse.

> *"Believer, the fountain of your joy is never dried up.*
> *If, like Jonah, your plants are withered (Jonah 4*
> *v 7), your God still lives. If, like Job, your goods*
> *have been plundered (Job 1 v 15), the highest good*
> *is still yours. Are the rivers dry? The ocean is full.*
> *Are the stars hidden? The heavenly sun shines on*
> *in eternal brightness. You have a possession that*
> *is unfading, a promise that is unfailing, and a*

Protector who is unchanging. Though you live in a
faithless world, you dwell in a faithful God."
(C.H. Spurgeon, Beside Still Waters, page 153)

In deep trials, Job learned more of who God was and is. Let the same be true of you as you navigate a difficult season. Let your marriage be a place where you learn more of who God is, rely on him, and press on in faith as you move toward the day when you will see Jesus. Let it be that when you get there, you can look back at your marriage as one that endured through trials, where you clung to Christ, encouraged each other, displayed Jesus, and came to see and know the unending faithfulness and goodness of God—together, through the storms.

REFLECT

- Have you been redeemed by the blood of Christ? If so, praise God that you are secure in him. If you haven't, what keeps you from turning to Jesus as your Lord, Savior, and Redeemer? Would you simply ask him to enable you not only to hear about him but to truly see him for who he is and how much blessing is found in him?

- What losses have you seen Christ restore or redeem in your life? Thank him for that! What areas do you desire to see him to restore? Pray and ask that God would restore these in his timing. What areas are impossible to restore in your lifetime? Share your grief with Christ and thank him that full restoration will one day come.

- (Together, if possible) Discuss what's most impacted you as you've read through each chapter. What's been challenging, what's been encouraging, and what has God taught you along the way? On your own or together, make a practical list of a few specific changes you'd like to work toward in your marriage and areas that you will commit to praying about. Share with each other what excites you and comforts you as you look forward to the restoration that is coming when Christ returns. If you're both willing to, pray together for restoration now, and then rejoice in the promised restoration that is coming!

PRAY

Jesus, thank you that you gave your life so that I could be redeemed and restored to you. Though I sometimes struggle to accept and understand the trials you have allowed in my life and marriage, thank you that you promise to work in and through them for my good and to one day restore and redeem every loss, tear, grief, and sorrow in your presence. As I have seen in the book of Job, you are sovereign, faithful, and good, even when I can't make sense of you or my circumstances. Jesus, I desire restoration now and I long for the restoration to come. Help me to trust you as I wait, and, like Job, allow me to experience the greatest joy and blessing— that of coming to see and know you like never before. Though you don't promise a perfect marriage now, please don't allow these trials to destroy our marriage but instead may they change us to be more like you— and to love, serve, and cherish each other as a result. Thank you that one day I will be able to look back in awe and gratitude for all you have done through these trials. In the meantime, please help us to walk stronger, together, through these storms. Amen.

For further meditation: Psalm 66 v 5-12, 16-20; Isaiah 54 v 4-14; Isaiah 57 v 18-19; Galatians 2 v 20; 3 v 13; 4 v 4-6.

Journaling

ACKNOWLEDGMENTS

First and foremost, we give all glory and honor to our Lord and Savior, Jesus Christ. Apart from his saving grace and faithful provision, not a word of this book would exist. May he alone be glorified in and through these pages.

Thank you to The Good Book Company for not only entrusting us with this opportunity but for allowing us to work alongside such an amazing group of talented, genuine, godly men and women. Each one of you are a gift to the body of Christ and a joy to work with.

There are very few words that can express our immense gratitude for Carl Laferton—our editor, brother in Christ, and friend. Thank you for your patience, wisdom, and graciousness, which made writing a book in one of the hardest seasons of life possible—dare we say, enjoyable. Not only did you make this a far better book than it ever could have been without you, but you have become a very dear friend to our family. We can't thank you enough for your continual encouragement and prayers throughout these difficult years. We will be forever grateful for you.

Of course, we couldn't write an acknowledgment without thanking our parents, who not only gave us life but raised us to know and love Jesus above all else. You have made sacrifices in ways that we will never fully understand and have led us by your profoundly impactful example of loving Christ and loving each other well, even when it hasn't been easy. Thank you for faithfully walking alongside us: grieving with us in our pain, rejoicing in our joys, praying for us when we had no words left of our own, and supporting us in ways that we will never be able to repay. Your love and support have carried us through more than you will ever know.

And to our children—Ben, Hannah, Haley, and Eli—thank you for your patience with us as we have sought to faithfully obey the Lord in writing these pages. We know that we are far from perfect parents and have not always been the example we desire to be, but we pray that you will always know how deeply we love you. Despite our failings, we pray that the Lord will open each of your eyes to see and know Jesus as your Lord and Savior, and that you will one day see how he will redeem and use every ounce of the pain and trials that you have been called to endure at such a young age. We are so proud of how you continue to persevere through the trials that many may never fully know or understand. May your lives be marked by the faithfulness, goodness, grace, hope, and joy of Christ.

We also want to thank Colin Smith, our pastor, mentor, and friend, who has faithfully preached God's word with wisdom and humility each and every week. You have taught us to be students of God's word and to study Scripture through the lens of the gospel. Thank you for encouraging me (Sarah) to start writing, which sent me on a journey that I never could have imagined, and for wisely counseling us as we embarked on writing this book together. And to the other pastors at the Orchard Evangelical Free Church, thank you for faithfully praying for, supporting, and encouraging us along the way.

Lastly, to our friends and family, who have prayed for and supported us each step of the way: though there are too many to thank personally, we are so grateful for your willingness to long-suffer with us through these past 12 years, faithfully praying, encouraging, and loving us, even when it was easy to grow weary. Whether it was a card, a meal, or the gift of sitting with us in our pain, you have continually shown us the love of Christ and the blessing of the body of Christ. We are profoundly thankful for each one of you and pray that you know how deeply loved you are.

BIBLICAL | RELEVANT | ACCESSIBLE

At The Good Book Company, we are dedicated to helping Christians and local churches grow. We believe that God's growth process always starts with hearing clearly what he has said to us through his timeless word—the Bible.

Ever since we opened our doors in 1991, we have been striving to produce Bible-based resources that bring glory to God. We have grown to become an international provider of user-friendly resources to the Christian community, with believers of all backgrounds and denominations using our books, Bible studies, devotionals, evangelistic resources, and DVD-based courses.

We want to equip ordinary Christians to live for Christ day by day, and churches to grow in their knowledge of God, their love for one another, and the effectiveness of their outreach.

Call us for a discussion of your needs or visit one of our local websites for more information on the resources and services we provide.

Your friends at The Good Book Company

thegoodbook.com | thegoodbook.co.uk
thegoodbook.com.au | thegoodbook.co.nz
thegoodbook.co.in